Thank you David!!

#IownUMP

90

Building The Ultimate Empire

MEL JONES

-Contents-

Look at a man the way he is and he only becomes worse,
but look at him as if he were what he could be,
then he becomes what he should be.
-Johann Wolfgang von Goethe

Introduction:
90 Days To The Top!

Every Empire has something in common. Throughout history, we see that each has had its own unique design and style yet every Empire ever built shared the same foundation. It was built on people. It was built on a number of cultivated and powerful minds all linked together for a common purpose. All directed in one direction. Each individual, no matter how one is different from the other, is synced with the vibration of the group. The people share one idea, with one goal in mind. The success of the Empire.

What is an Empire? It can range anywhere from a government, a kingdom, a country, a tribe, a corporation, a business, a school, a sports team, a family, or even a person. An Empire is something strong and powerful. It breathes untouchable. An Empire is vast and scalable. It is creative and adaptive. An Empire is always on the offensive, building and enlarging its forces. In turn, that offense becomes its defense. The unstoppable object becomes the impenetrable force. A true Empire is well-known, well-respected, and profoundly efficient. And though many Empires have surfaced across this great green earth, they all had the same starting point. Someone's mind.

Why is this important? What does this mean to you? It means everything in the world to you, because currently you are building an Empire. At this very moment you are creating something. Unfortunately, most of us don't know it, so we end up building a hut instead of a 1000 foot tall sky scraper. Many get so beat down mentally that they never see what is possible for them. All they can see is the millions of poorly finished huts being overshadowed by the few who decided to build Kingdoms worthy enough to be called home. But I'm not here to rain on your parade nor am I here to motivate you to do better. This book wasn't written to inspire you to become more or to become your best. I wrote this book to help you, the motivated and purpose driven individuals, to construct your Empire.

Wait, I forgot. Empires fall, don't they? Empires have weaknesses. Empires have a life span and no matter how the cards are dealt, no matter what lady luck has offered you, your Empire will fall eventually. Why? Because those who are born of this world must also die in it. When the King and Queen expires, so does their reign. That's ok. The goal is not to live forever. It is to experience paradise while you live. It is to create an ever growing, ever changing, ever adapting, and ever improving creature. It is a living entity. It is not perfect and neither will you ever be. The major key to capture on this journey is to find a way to not only manifest your Empire, but to uncover the secret to building the Ultimate Empire.

This is for the CEO who is redefining what it means to be a supporting member of the company. The manager who has to not only deal with their own problems, but also the mental paralysis that plagues their subordinates when change comes rearing its ugly head around the corner.

This is for the mother trying to make ends meet for her family. Working on not only paying the bills, but creating an income that will create a financially stress free environment for her family.

This is for the husband trying to re-establish the

marriage. The father trying to build a strong communication between him and his kids. The son trying to re-affirm pride in his parents. The sister trying to reconnect with her siblings.

This is not a 90 day challenge, this is a life challenge. This is a manual to understanding yourself. To understanding how greatness thinks and what negative thoughts must be destroyed. This is so you can Master the Art of Powerful Thinking. *90: Building The Ultimate Empire* is a window into a person's soul. A window we all try to keep shut and hide from the rest of the world. In order to build the Ultimate Empire you must know what your greatest asset is all about. People.

Now, you can read this book over a course of 90 days, chapter by chapter, internalizing these ideas and Mastering the Art of Powerful Thinking one day at a time. Or you can read it all in one day. It's up to you. I would say that neither way is more effective than the other overall. It really all depends on where you are in life. What kind of student you are. What you goal is in life. What you want your life to look like. The point is to just understand which areas of your thinking you are lacking in. Those are the chapters that will stand out the most to you. The next step is to understand the mental faculties that your people are struggling in. Whether that be your kids, your spouse, your teammates, your employees, your peers, your business partners, or even your boss. The better you understand yourself, the better you will understand people. The greater your mastery is over your thoughts, the more successful you will be in life.

You are at war. A war between the current you and the upgrade you desire to upload. A greater you. A better you. And that future you holds the keys to your legacy. What will your legacy be? An unfinished hut built on fear and ignorance, or will it be the idea that you were successful in building the Ultimate Empire?

Chapter 1
Take Action

Did you know that taking action is the first and last step to building the Ultimate Empire? It's also the second and third step. Even the fourth and the fifth. Now you're starting to get it, it's the only step. ACTION, ACTION, ACTION. That's why they say your actions dictate your future. It's what you do. Even when you don't do something, you're really doing something else. So the question then becomes, what are you doing?

What makes a salesman so effective? What makes them successful? We know that they're usually effective communicators. Typically they ask the right questions. They listen intently and can regurgitate what was said. They have the ability to connect with potential customers. Man or woman, does not matter. Big or small is irrelevant. Even race is a non-factor. The skills that a salesman holds affect their ability to make a sale. But what I have come to find is that having a particular skill set does not build you the Ultimate Empire. Meaning, it will not make you the top salesman. It will make you good, but not great. The only thing that can do that is the amount of action you take per day. What you physically do. How much you promote yourself, your brand, and how many people you attempt to sell. Period.

But this is not a secret. This is not a hidden or mysterious strategy that only the rich know about. Almost every single person on the planet realizes this truth, and almost everyone follows this rule from time to time. But not all the time. And that's what separates the good from the great.

What happens to the wife who gives up on her troubled teen? What happens to the husband who stops trying to make his wife happy? What happens to the company that doesn't adapt to the times? What happens to the student that doesn't look for a tutor to get his grades up? You know what happens. But why does it happen? Because they chose to take action in a different direction. That's it.

Right now you're reading a book bent on peaking your self-awareness. This is your current action. When you are done, you will make a choice. You will either choose to progress or ignore. You will work on that area of your life that is hurting your Empire. Not because you know you will succeed, but because you know that option is available, making your desired result possible. Or you will do something irrelevant, maybe detrimental to your success. This decision is purely based on how motivated you are for change.

You know what separates Napoleon Hill from every other author of his time. Nothing. They all took action in writing books. They all did their research and made their analysis. They all were creative and organized. They all took the time to write whether they felt like it or not. There was nothing special about Napoleon Hill, he just took action toward the course of his dreams. He could have easily done otherwise. It's like they say, "it's easy to do, and easy not to do." What will you do?

Will you finish this book? Will you share it? Will

you begin writing your own? I don't know, nobody knows. You probably don't even know, but I know you will do something. And when you do it a reaction will follow. Usually that reaction falls in line with what you did. Maybe its criticism, maybe it's failure, or maybe you'll hit the jackpot. The point is not to convince you to take action. Like you, I just want to know what your next move will be. The responsibility is yours and it always will be.

Chapter 2
Get Started

The most common threat to your Empire is the inability to get started. To get started reading, to get started making calls,, to get started on your book, to get started on networking, to get started on advertising, to get started making your product or whatever it may be. The average human being will speak of the change that they wish to implement into their life, but they never get started on it. People talk of improving their fitness but never join a gym or worse, they join and never start an exercise routine. I've seen it happen time and time again. You've seen it yourself, you've even been a participant. Don't be embarrassed, so have I.

I remember so many times in school I would stay up late until the last minute to study for an exam, read an assignment, or do my homework. The worst is when I would start preparing to do my projects the day before it was due. It was not until then when I would realize that the project required materials that I didn't have in my possession. It needed information that I didn't research. It required certain steps that would normally take 2-3 days to complete. This is what happens when you procrastinate. This is an example of what happens when you wait to get started. Life sneaks up on you and presents you with a challenge you're not ready for because you waited. Are you waiting to start building the Ultimate Empire?

What if you wait to get started with your marriage counseling because you want to make sure your numbers look good this year for work? Or maybe you want to wait until after the football season. Or maybe you want to wait until your husband is done with school. What if you read all the books on great pickup lines so you could ask a particular girl out on a date and kept putting it off because you wanted to do more research? What if you waited so long that somebody else asked her out instead? What if they started dating? What if Steve Jobs never started Apple because he felt they weren't ready? What if....

Here's the most important question. Why don't people get started? Why don't they get going? Why don't they begin to change their habits and become more productive employees? Why don't they begin to show their kids more attention? Why don't they start that company? For obvious reasons: fear, doubt, uncertainty, and insecurity.

Where does this fear and doubt stem from? From the belief that they lack something. Lack money, lack experience, lack education, lack resources, lack time, lack ability, lack a network, lack the right and some just lack motivation. So, by identifying your "lack of" you can now combat that belief with evidence of what you actually have and need.

Lacking money is irrelevant. If you follow Entrepreneurial Guru's like Gary Vaynerchuk, you will find that though it may be difficult to get a loan from a bank these days, it is more than accessible to obtain money from investors. Lack of experience only pertains to graduating school. When it comes to playing football, freshman are brought in every year to colleges all over

America to start playing right off the bat. The coach doesn't care about experience; they just want to know can you play. Lack of education is a problem for becoming a school teacher, but it means nothing when it comes to starting a business. Henry Ford had no high school education yet he still built the giant we know today as Ford Motor Company from scratch. Lack of resources used to be true back before the Internet. But now we live in a time where if you need help finding a way to do, get, or learn something all you have to do is Google the answer. Lack of time means an unlimited source of excuses. Did you know that each of us is blessed with the same amount of time to complete our mission every day? No one person's 24 hours is any longer than yours. No one has a time machine and no one is allotted a shortcut on time. Everyone on the planet has to figure out how to get things done in 24 hours every day. Some people are creating their Ultimate Empire inside of that 24, while others are wishing they had more time to do so.

Lack of ability is nonsense. We were all born as infants with no ability to walk and talk. We each had to learn that. Sure some of us are genetically gifted, but if talent don't work hard, hard work will beat talent. If the genius doesn't show up to class, she will never get into college. If the 6'8" basketball player doesn't play defense, then he probably won't play. Simple as that. Lacking a network is normal because most people don't have friends. Most people have never met a business owner. Most people have never worked with other employees. Most people don't have favorite spots to hang out with. Most people only know their immediate family and never venture out into the world to see who else is living in it.

Does this sound like you? Does this sound like a normal person's life? I think it's safe to say you know all of these type of people. I think the problem is maybe you feel like you don't have the right to live a happier life. Maybe you feel like you don't deserve to make more money. Maybe you feel like you're not supposed to do something fulfilling. Maybe you feel like inadequacy is your punishment for not being born the right person or making the wrong decisions in the past. It's a good thing Martin Luther King Jr. didn't feel that way. Or Eric Thomas, or J.K. Rowling, or Stephen Hawking's, or Oprah.

Lack of motivation. If you're letting your fear of "lack" get in the way of your destiny or halt your progress then you just lack the pure motivation to overcome. Not that you don't want it, you just don't want it bad enough to fall on your face and fail because ultimately that has to happen sometimes. Not all the time, but sometimes. But as you know failing is all a part of the process of building your Ultimate Empire. So, if fear of "lack" is what is holding you back, your family back, your relationship back, or your company back, then you must ask what is that motivating factor that is missing? You figure that out and you will have no problem getting things started.

If I kept telling people that I wanted to be a motivational speaker one day but never got started on my dream, then I wouldn't be a 25 year old Black Male speaking on YouTube, building a followship on Instagram and Snapchat, and doing venues for schools and businesses. If I had let fear of experience and money get in my way, this book would not have been written. The very idea probably would have never come to mind. Why? Because a mind stuck in inaction cannot envision anything greater for itself. Get started today.

Chapter 3
Commitment

It's not difficult for human beings to commit. Oh no, we commit to all kinds of things. In fact, commitment may be our strongest trait. Yes, humans are very committed, very committed to what they know. Very committed to what they are used too. Very committed to what is safe and familiar. We tend to eat the same most days, drink the same, talk about the same subjects, complain about the same people, work at the same job, drive down the same roads, and even hang with the same people. Yes, you are indeed very committed to your way of life, even to your own personality. There is no mistaking your commitment. Where man falls is in his inability to commit to something new.

We don't change for the most part. People don't want to have to adapt to a new lifestyle, or a new boss, or maybe a new system. It throws them off. Makes them feel uncomfortable because new means uncertainty. And everyone wants to be certain. Well I want you to be certain that the only thing constant in the universe is change. Life is constantly moving, growing, dying, and expanding. People are being born every day, as well as passing away. Right now, cells in your body are multiplying and dying off. People's personalities are maturing and developing. You will not be the same person yesterday as you were today. Then why must you try to hang on to what you once were?

22

I know you are capable of committing, but to what? Are you willing to commit to your diet? Are you willing to commit to your new start up? Are you willing to commit to finishing this book? Will you commit to seeing your children? It's not hard nor impossible. But it is different from what you normally do.

Being committed to your normal activities will most likely give you the same expected outcome day in day out. So if you are committed to executing dream oriented tasks, you will get at least one step closer to your dreams every day. The day I found out I was going to be a father was the Summer I made the ultimate commitment to be the type of father my son could be proud of. At the time I was going into my junior year at the College of William and Mary. I played running back for the Tribe Football team and went from no scholarship to half. I was living in an apartment by myself because my roommate had just moved out after graduating in the spring. I had no bed at the time because he took that with him. No laptop because mine was out of commission. No car, a new phone plan separate from my parents, and of course I had to feed myself. Did I mention that I was training with the football team that summer Monday through Friday from 6 am to 9am? I had a lot to take care of in a 3 month span before pre-season camp started up. So I did what any responsible and determined 20 year old college student would do in my situation, I committed to the GRIND.

I was already working a job as a car wash attendant during the spring. That was enough to pay my rent and feed myself. But I needed to get a car, laptop, and bed before the summer was over. So I committed to 2 more jobs. One as a bouncer and another doing light maintenance and event set up for W&M. I ended up averaging between 70 - 80 hours a week on the clock for 3 solid months and still managed to wake up every day for 6am workouts. I was hungry.

What came of my efforts? By the end of the summer, I bought a car, a new bed, and a new Mac Book. I paid my rent, my utilities, and my phone bill. I fed myself every day and I did all of this sleeping an average of 2-4 hours a night. I was committed.

Human beings are committed for one of 2 reasons. Either because it's safe and that's what they know best or they are motivated by their desire to have. If you want something you don't have you must be willing to do something that you've never done. And you can't just do it for one day. You can't just do it a few times. You have to stick it out until the end. You have to commit to that action every day until it's done. But you will only do that if you're motivated to have it. If you feel like the prize is worth it. If you believe you can do it. If you can see yourself making it happen, then you will commit to change.

Anybody can commit to anything, but only somebody inspired by possibilities for themselves will commit to building the ultimate Empire brick by brick.

Chapter 4
Dedication

I've been reading a lot of self-development books, listening to a lot of motivational speakers, and watching a ton of video on success. And I've come to notice that they are all saying the same thing. Even knowing this though, I continue to listen, read, and watch the latest and greatest. Why? Because I understand the power of brainwashing.

Here's the deal, we are all brainwashed. I know, you're probably one of those one in a million folks out there who are immune to any type of brainwashing and are completely individualistic in their being. You're different. That's cute, but let me tell you that you're not anyone special. You're just another pawn in the system, playing victim to this big bad world. Whatever you choose to do, someone's already done a version of it. Whatever you believe in, you learned from someone else. From the clothes you buy to the technology you indulge in, it is all based on what somebody else has convinced you to do. Whether it's coincidental or not, we have all been brainwashed. What you come into contact with the most will most influence your mind and life choices. This is why I expose myself to more of the same material every day, because I know it is transforming my mind to think in the most productive, positive, and loving way.

I am dedicated to improvement. Dedication is the same as commitment. They mean exactly the same thing, but I wanted to instill this idea in your head so in case it went over your head the chapter before, you may catch it the second time. Dedication is resilience. It is a resolve to do whatever is required to win. Dedication is proof to you that I am willing to do what it takes to make you better so that your life will be better.

Here is what dedication brought me that commitment could not. A cool acronym. D is for **desire**. Desire is deeper than want. Desire means you can't go home without it. It means you want something as bad as you want to breathe. E is for **excellence**. No one became phenomenal from doing something great one time. Being successful means you take full responsibility of everyday and each day is held to a high standard. The high standard is excellence. Excellence is what things look like when you do them right and professionally. Next is D, **drive**. It's that thing that makes you tick. It's that push and that edge you need. It's that passion inside of you. Your drive is your fuel. Your reason for grinding will drive you to fight for what you deserve. I is for **independence**. You don't need someone to hold your hand, but you will gladly accept assistance. You don't need someone to instruct you on what to do next, you look for what needs to be done. Independence means you will work on your Ultimate Empire whether someone is by your side or not. C is for **compete**. This is what the big companies are doing, but is something the small people lack. The will to compete. The desire to win. The drive to do the most sales in the office. The need to be your child's number one role model. The ambition to be that next big company. The ability to fight the barriers and annihilate the competition.

A is for **action**. Self-explanatory, but rarely self-applied. You can tell me you're dedicated to serving your

26

wife, but will you do it. Will you change your habits to please her? Will you stay up an extra hour to massage her feet? Will you turn off the TV to listen to her talk about her day? Action. Empires are built by laying the bricks one at a time, not talking about it. T is **time**. Using your time wisely. Finding time to develop new skills. Taking time to learn new strategies. Taking time to connect with yourself. Time. It is our most precious commodity that we can never get back. Will you dedicate yourself to making every minute count or will you dedicate time to chance. I is for **inspire**. 1) You must re-inspire yourself every day and 2) you must inspire your team, company, partner, or family.

This is what a Powerful Thinking Coach like myself is for, not to tell you how to do it, but to explain to you how it's been done time and time again in the worst of conditions. To inspire you, get your creative juices flowing. Listen to the greats whenever you're in your car. Speakers like Zig Ziglar, Les Brown, Eric Thomas, Jim Rohn, Tony Robins, Brendon Burchard, Grant Cardone and Gary Vaynerchuk. They will get your motor fired up. Then take that same energy and pour it into someone else's life. Into your teams life so you may become one. Into your company so that you may expand horizons. Into your partner so that you may grow together. And into your family so that your bond may strengthen ever tighter. O is your **opponent**. Knowing your opponent will always give the chance to fight. If you don't know who you're fighting, why would you fight? Your biggest opponent is the old you. The you that needs work. The you that is not all that you wish to be. The you that desires more out of life. You have to defeat the old you today and every day. Each day that you win is a success and if you win enough days you will be called successful. The last is N is for **no negativity**. There is no need and no room. Negativity is the exact opposite of dedication and all it stands for. It goes against each letter and will destroy your Empire before it ever has a chance to stand. Negativity truly is the devils work.

Many people are dedicated to something or someone, the real question is what or who? Is it something worthwhile or is it to someone negative? Dedication just needs proper direction. If you can direct that energy towards your dreams, your goals, and your ambitions, how could you not become successful? Whatever you want in life, whatever you're trying to build, whoever you're trying to lead, if you stay dedicated to your cause and not to distractions then you will always succeed.

Chapter 5
Practice

They say practice makes perfect, or improvement, or better, or whatever. You know what it really does. Practice makes life not fun. Practice can sometimes be a living hell. Practice is a sorry excuse for losers who need more time to prepare for battle. Practice is lame. Practice is necessary. To be a champion practice is required.

I've been practicing for a long time. So have you. Since day one you have been practicing for tomorrow. You have been putting in the hours, talking to the people, making the calls, listening to your kids, writing the essays, giving the presentations, lifting the weights, running the sprints, owning up to your mistakes. And for what, a chance to get it perfect tomorrow. But you can never be perfect, so why even bother taking the time to practice your craft. Because no one else is perfect either, so you always have a shot.

Talent is talent. It is beautiful and majestic. It is seemingly effortless. Practice seems to be irrelevant to talent. But what good is athletic talent if you can't stay eligible to play? What good is intellectual talent if you're knowledgeable about the wrong subject? Steve Jobs had no real talent. But he had direction. He had focus and he had drive. He was committed to perfection. Though he knew one could never reach it, he still practiced getting there.

To be a Steph Curry and sink 77 three pointers in a row, you have to be a work-a-holic. You would have to master the game of basketball. And that is the true meaning of practice, Mastery. Mastery is total awareness of all basic knowledge, strategies, and techniques within a particular field or industry. It is complete control over all necessary participating faculties of your mind and body. It is the idea of things becoming second nature. The only thing you consciously think about is winning. All you focus on is the next move. Losing can't be taken seriously. Losing is something only the unprepared think about. Those who have not put in enough practice. Winning is the only thing on the mind of someone who has reached a level of Mastery. Practicing is the art of attaining Mastery.

But most people do not enjoy the struggles of practicing. In fact, most loathe its necessity. As do I, yet I spend each day practicing to become a better coach, speaker, writer, father, lover, son, brother, mentor, student, listener, and communicator. Why? Because most won't, and that's what gives me an edge. Why? Because most refuse, and that directly correlates to their mediocre lives. Why? Because the greats do and I want to be great, just like you do. But you cannot build the Ultimate Empire on your own. You need other great people to help you. You will find these people through practice. Practicing the search, practicing the interviews, practicing teaching, practicing inspiring, and practicing leading.

Your team won't do it unless you do it. And if they do, it will be short lived. The Ultimate Empire is not a set standard across the board, it is your standard. It is what you dream of and how you see yourself living. It is your desires and your best, and how will you ever see your best unless you practice giving your best every day?

Chapter 6
Preparation-H

Game plan? I only have one game plan, code named Preparation - Hustle. In other words, prepare to hustle. Can I keep it real with you? I've been building my dream of becoming a world class speaker for a little over 2 years now. Before that, I spent 17 years chasing my childhood dream of becoming an NFL player. And you know what I have learned in these 25 years of immense life experience? People are terrified of the **Hustle**.

When I speak of hustle, I don't mean running. I'm not talking exercise. It's not about how many jobs you have or how many hours you clocked in. You don't have to be an entrepreneur or write a book. When I say hustle, I'm talking about working on your dreams and goals. I mean doing what others won't, to become what others aren't and get what most don't have. Hustle is putting in the extra work when no one is watching. Hustle is grinding when you're not sure if it's going to work. Hustle is doing what you're scared to do. Hustle is doing whatever is required to match your goals because that is what you set out to do. Prepare to Hustle.

Sam Walton, one of the ultimate hustlers of our time, started out as a young man with the goals of running a successful variety store in Newport, Arkansas. That dream slowly developed into something a lot bigger known as the Super Giant Discount Retailer called Wal-Mart. This now

11,000 store chain operates in 28 countries including Canada, Mexico, United Kingdom and Japan. It is the world's largest company by revenue and is the biggest private employer in the world with 2.2 million employees. But Sam Walton started with just one store in little old Rogers, Arkansas. With nothing but a dollar, a dream, and his preparation to hustle, Sam grew his company to 24 stores reaching $12.6 million in sales within the first 5 years. That's with no rich parents, no network, no handouts, and no support but the support of his vision. He was willing to do whatever it took to make his dream become a reality. He was willing to take on the super giants of the retail world, competing in a way that had never been seen before. From popcorn makers to live bands in the parking lot, Sam made sure he got the traffic necessary to build his Ultimate Empire.

Hustle. It's more than work, it's an attitude. Hustlers don't take no for an answer. To them no means maybe and it is up to them to turn that maybe into a yes. Hustlers don't just work hard when it's easy, they GRIND even when things seem impossible. Anybody can put in the work when they are winning. Few will give it their all when the chips are down. Most will quit before they ever get started. Why? Because it's too hard. They don't know how to do something. No one showed them how. They don't have any extra money. People said they couldn't do it. You want to write a Best Seller, get to hustling.

If you're not a hustler then how can you expect for your kids to be? If you're not a hustler, how do you expect your team to be? If you are not a hustler, your employees won't believe you and customers will ignore you. The world respects the hustle, so be prepared to get out there and get it.

Chapter 7
Research

You can't go through school without doing it. As you rise through the ranks from first grade all the way through high school and College, research is steadily expected of you more and more. It's a way of life. It's the only way to complete your projects and tasks. You must research events throughout history, important people, scientific findings, and statistical information. No way around it, you can only go through it. And we shouldn't try to go around it for it is essential to our medical system, economic system, defense system, and overall human evolution. But we only tend to do it when it is required by our job or class curriculum. What about life outside of the system?

How does one become spiritually more inclined with their God or deity? By studying the handbook. For Christians it's the Bible. For Muslims it's the Quran. How else do you expect to gain a deeper understanding of your faith if you do not research the book written on the subject? It seems like it would be almost impossible to do so. So why does society not research success once they have graduated? Why don't we research things outside of our jobs necessity? How about our health, finances, investing, meditation, other faiths, herbs, medicine, government, business, love, sex, and happiness. How about reading up on how to sell people, on how to connect deeper with your spouse, on the history of medicine, or on different styles of exercise. We should all take time out of our day to study up on some particular subject that will allow us to make more efficient decisions in our lives. Why? Because none of us were born perfect, so there is always room for improvement.

I heard once that Warren Buffet spends the first 6 hours of his day, every day, reading. Reading what? Reading financial statements. Reading up on business. Reading about a company's past success. Reading up on economic strategies and business techniques. Reading up on stocks and the market. Even though he is one the top 5 richest men in the world, he makes reading a priority. He still put's in ridiculous research time as if he were ignorant on the subject of business and money. Don't you understand? The biggest Empires in the world, the most successful people in life have dedicated themselves to a lifelong education. And if we have learned anything about education, that's researching the subject matter.

Where does it all start? It starts with you. You have to put in the time every day to learn. You have to dedicate your life to self-education. You have to do the research. Before you apply for a job, you research what the company and position is about. Before you buy a car, you look up reviews and ask family members about it. Before you pick a college, you visit the campus. Before you retire for tonight, download a bit of information that will take your game to the next level. That will improve your skills. That will upgrade your interactions with people. The more you do that, the more of the right kind of people will be attracted to you. The more likely your circle of influence will be motivated to grow and learn. The more value you will be able to provide to people's lives and the more value they will want to reciprocate. The law of attraction. Like attracts like. Upgrades attract more upgrades. Take your Empire to the next level. Do your research.

Chapter 8
Lack There Of

We now live in a time where the term "lack" should no longer be an issue. We have more than enough food, more than enough energy, more than enough water, and more than enough money. We have the knowledge, the man power, and the expertise to create and build whatever we want. Man has gone to the moon and now has set his sights on the universe. We have even established a universal method of communication that can simultaneously connect everyone on earth to a continuous stream of information in the form of audio, video, and writing that is constantly being added to in a space that has unlimited space as well as potential. You may know of it as the Internet.

We have phones so advanced that we call them smart. Watches that have evolved from the function of time keepers and have stepped into a realm that can easily be categorized as wrist computers. School itself is becoming less and less relevant, for anything you could possibly want to learn about has been put into a book. All human knowledge and history has been written and recorded. We have the tools, we have the information, and we have access to anything and everything. Especially in America, the land of milk and honey, where so many native born citizens play victim in a society where all the tools necessary have been handed to them (Or at least placed within their vicinity). Here you can be rich by choice or poor by choice. You can choose to live in a mansion or sleep road under the bridge instead. You can raise a family of 5 or live alone. You want to be the CEO of a Fortune 500 company. There's a blueprint for how to do that. You have options. And each option requires a particular action from you.

Money seems to be people's biggest complaint for why they cannot build their dreams. As if we lack of it. According to the Federal Reserve, there is approximately $1.39 trillion in circulation as of September 30, 2015. And guess what, most people are complaining about the lack of it. Most people are playing the victim and hoping that one day it all will coming crashing into their homes. Like a wave of entitlement, they wait for that first billion to come pouring into their lives because that is the only way anybody gets wealthy. They would put in the conscious effort to do so but there are too many impossible obstacles standing in their way that no one else has ever had to go through. Out of the billions of people that have ever existed, their experiences are completely unique and unheard of. And what it ultimately always boils down to is "lack."

Lack of money, lack of time, lack of knowledge, lack of a network, lack of a market, lack of proof, lack of motivation, even lack of need. How legit are these lacks?

Lack of Money: John Paul Jones DeJoria started Paul Mitchell Hair Care Products with only $700 dollars to his name and is now a Billionaire. Eric Thomas quit his six figure job to do videos for FREE on YouTube while giving speeches at schools for a few hundred dollars at a time. He is now one of the top 5 speakers in the world. And now a days, if you have a great App idea or business venture with an impressive presentation you can get investors to fund your passion, because everybody is looking for their next Mark Zuckerberg.

Lack of Time: We all have 24 hours. Scientist have concluded this as a worldwide fact. It cannot and will not be altered for anybody ever. Yet Curtis "50cent" Jackson found a way to film a movie and record the soundtrack to it at the same time. Yet Grant Cardone wrote his first book and best-seller in a day. And yet President Obama, who holds the most important and demanding position imaginable, still finds the time to raise a family and be a loving spouse to his wife.

Lack of Knowledge: I told you before, a book has been written on every subject matter imaginable. You don't need to go to college to learn it, the book is available to all. And there are subjects that a University won't teach you. Subjects on love, parenting, and success are lacking in the classroom, but are abundant inside of any library. On top of that Google and YouTube will give us any answer at the click of a button. Instantly you can download information that will tell you exactly what you need to know to build your Empire.

Lack of a Network: There are over 7 Billion people on this planet, and you are telling me you can't find anyone on it with the connection that you need? Are you telling me that there is no one out there looking for someone with your skills or talents? Are you saying that there is no one out there looking to provide you with the service you need? Is it possible that some people are just too scared to talk to strangers or even people they know? Like that girl every boy in school is afraid to talk to because she is so drop dead gorgeous. You don't need a network, you need some guts.

Lack of a Market: There was a time when the thought of computers being in people's homes was deemed as ridiculous and implausible at best. Back when Steve Jobs and Bill Gates first began building their brands. Now, it is odd if a household doesn't have at least one computer somewhere in it. Almost as odd as not having a TV. It's a parent trying to sell their child on the idea that school is important. They won't buy it until they see the value in it. If you can bring value into the equation, there is always a market for what you have.

Lack of Proof: Everyone wants proof that something will work. And when they get it, they still won't go through with it because they can't see it working for them. The husband won't go to marriage counseling, the mother won't let her son become a musician, the single man won't join the network marketing company, the High School girl won't put her clothing designs on social media. Though countless of others before have been successful in these realms, many fall under the trap that it can't happen for them. They have the proof right in front of them but it's blocked by their vision of seeing their own failure.

Lack of motivation and need: If you lack the motivation to create a unique lifestyle for yourself, then you simply don't see the need to live it. You don't have the urgency to change your life for the better. Anyone who is living their dreams is doing so because they saw it as a necessity. They believed they needed to have that career. They believed they were meant for that type of family. They felt they fully deserved that house. They could not live another day not doing what they love and believe in.

As long as people lack the need, they will lack the motivation to grind for something better. They will have no interest in becoming more. You build the Ultimate Empire through motivation, because it is impossible to lack any other physical element in this natural reality. Anything and everything you could possibly want is here, it just has to be a need for you to get it.

Chapter 9
Plan

They say those who fail to plan, plan to fail. After experiencing life through the lens of planning and taking pre-mature action, I have come to find that grinding without a specific plan is not the end of the world. In fact, many people spend all of their lives planning and never jump into the water. They never get on the field; they just keep drawing up plans and strategies without ever testing them out. Those who succeed in planning, yet fail to take action are even worse off than the gun slingers. At least the A-type personalities give themselves a chance to stumble upon the right way to win. Now here is something more interesting. Planning is an action as well that most people are too scared or lazy to ever exercise.

Assuming that you, your team, your company, your family and your friends are currently action takers or are in the process of taking action, I will explain to you why those who fail to plan usually plan to fail. It is because a captain that sets sail to a destination with no plan on how he will get there will surely get the ship and the crew lost at sea. It's great to have courage and go into battle, but without a plan on how one will attack the enemy and protect it's home front, the war will surely be lost before it ever begun. Action is the birth of success and planning is the doctor that guides it.

More than 2 years ago I decided, after doing one video for my first YouTube channel that I was going to become a World Class Motivational Speaker. That was it. There was no more to be said and no other questions to be asked. I had taken the first step towards my dream by posting my first, really bad, motivational message to the world. What was the next step? I had to plan. I was already willing to take action and I proved it, but now I needed some sort of series of steps to get me to my dream. So I thought about how my secret mentor, Eric Thomas, went from being homeless on the street to being one of the top five motivational speakers in the world. CONTENT. Lots and lots of content. He had put up hundreds of inspirational videos onto YouTube, thousands of motivating messages onto Twitter and Facebook. So it only made sense to me to focus my energy on providing loads of content. So I decided from there I would put up 90 videos in 90 days, to improve my speaking abilities quicker, and then continue to post periodically for better quality. I also started a blog, on BlogSpot at the time, and planned out the same strategy. I figured I couldn't just rely on the internet to get my name out there and build my credibility, so I decided to quit my then current job as a waiter and part time tree-slayer (arborist), to become a Personal Trainer. That way I could make more money, spend less time working, and network with hundreds of different people with many unique connections and backgrounds. The third phase was to commit to a lifetime of reading self-development books and listening to motivational messages while driving. Safe to say, my plan worked.

Did it make me a world class speaker the next day? No! Did it make all of my dreams come true overnight? Of course not. Did this plan eliminate the need for struggle and grind to build my dream one stone at a time? Wouldn't that have bene nice, but no. What it did do was point my life in the right direction. It allowed me to more than double my income. It gave me a chance to speak to multiple businesses, schools, non-profits, radio stations, and sports teams. It gave me a lane to focus all of my energy on. It gave me a voice in the mass clutter of information that is social media. My plan did not create my dreams, it gave me the tools for me to build them.

Your business cannot grow if there is not a plan in place on how it is going to be done. Your family cannot grow closer if you don't know how to do it. Your fitness ambitions will dwindle if you spend every day shooting from the hip and never get a plan in place on how you are going to achieve the desired results. Action will get the ball rolling and you will be commended for it, but when the fires dies out you must have a plan in place to follow. One that you can go back to when times get hectic and confusing. Plan accordingly and plan while you are doing. Plan to win. Plan the Ultimate Empire.

Chapter 10
Your Goals

I remember a colleague of mine was getting ready to depart from the company we worked for. She was the Fitness Director (Head Personal Trainer) of the gym and I a Personal Trainer. We had one final meeting as a Personal Trainer staff and in that meeting our Fitness Director shared stories about each of us and what she believed to be our greatest attribute. As she got around to me I was wondering what she would say. Would she tell of how positive I am? Maybe how friendly and interactive I am with the gym members. Maybe she would speak on how hard I work and helpful I am to staff. When my colleague got to me, she was able to sum up exactly what made me a winner. She said, "Mel. If I could some you up in two words, I would say GOAL ORIENTED."

What are your goals this year? How about this summer? Maybe just this month? If we broke it down to this week, what would be your end of the week goal? What do you plan on achieving today? What do you want to get out of this hour and this book? What are your goals?

Do you know what LeBron James' goal is every year at the end of the last season? To win an NBA championship the next season. Now, he might not always do it, but he's usually pretty close. What are most people doing instead? Thinking about the weekend or how they are going to get through this day. That's it. Two people can be

44

partners in the same company. One could be fixed on the idea of staying afloat and making sure sales don't decline, while the other may be focused on doubling revenue next year. They both have considerable interest in the company yet they're goals are different. What are your goals?

Maybe you are one of those people who doesn't have any goals. Maybe you are one of those folks who don't like to have goals because you don't want to disappoint yourself. Maybe you are embarrassed to create a goal that other people may laugh at. Whatever your reasoning may be, I want you to know that even the least goal oriented people have goals in life. It might be to pay rent this month or keep from having a heart attack. Goals are goals. And very importantly, what you see is what you get.

If you don't know what you want then you will receive things you were not expecting to get. Could be health issues, financial problems, or even marital troubles. Maybe your kids are on drugs. I don't know what it is for you, but I do know even if you think your mind is blank from a goal, it is always fixed on something consciously and subconsciously.

Law of attraction. It's about manifesting into your life what you focus on most. That does not mean that pure thought will create riches for you, yet if you focus on something intensely enough your mind will begin to create and see opportunities for achieving the focused destination. Your body will begin to act in ways that correspond with those opportunities. Your most dominant thoughts will lead you. Your most dominant goals will take you in that direction. Your body must put in the work, but your mind must know the x on the spot. Even if you don't initially know how to get there, thinking, attempting, and asking questions will slowly draw the necessary map needed to get you to your goals.

Relationships usually fail not because of boredom or time, but because of the couple's lack of goal setting. Getting married is easy, because when it becomes your goal in life to reach marital bliss then your mind finds a way to get there. You act accordingly to get someone to fall in love with you so that you can get officially hitched before they get back up. What happens next, usually, is you have kids and then work for the rest of your life. That's it. You have reached the top. The thing you've been preparing for all your life begins and ends at 25. Life as a mindless Zombie begins and life as a creator of destiny ends. But it doesn't have to, and it shouldn't ever be that way. My colleague didn't recognize something special about me, she just pointed me out as a goal-getter. I've' always had big goals, even when I was 7 years old. I had goals of being a top notch running back for Virginia Tech and going to the NFL. I ended up playing for William and Mary in Williamsburg, VA instead. It wasn't Tech, but it was close.

The Ultimate Empire is goal oriented. That's what keeps it going. That's what keeps it growing. The fire that burns inside is the logs of goals burning in the fireplace. The only way to complete those goals is to GRIND every day until they are burned up. Then it is time to throw in another batch. Now set your goals and fuel your Empire.

Chapter 11
Fear

It is deadliest and most destructive human emotion on the face of the planet. It has torn down cities and wiped out civilizations. It has poisoned the minds of men and has led astray an entire generation. FEAR. Fear is the very opposite of love. You know what's funny about fear, it cannot exist in the same space as love. Like light cannot occupy the same room as darkness, one must drive the other out. There is no room for both. So why does man fear an all loving God?

There are 2 causes of fear I would like to address. There are plenty of other causes, but they are not of my concern. When it comes to building the Ultimate Empire, there are two very specific fears that will halt your plans if you do not handle them with care and expediency. They are Fear of Failure and Fear of Consequence.

The first fear is the most prominent and talked about. The Fear of Failure. No one wants to fail. Even those who say failing is the fastest way to success and promote failing often to become better, even they don't enjoy the process. We all want to win. We want to succeed. We want that business to run smoothly. We want our family to be happy. We want our spouse to love us. We want our health to be strong. We want our fitness to be impressive. We want our mind to be sharp. We want our tongue to be quick and our pen to be swift. There is nothing more satisfying than success, but the fear of failure overshadows the thought of that possibility.

How many times did Thomas Edison fail trying to invent the light bulb? I don't know, thousands of times. How many vendors said no to Kernel Sanders before somebody finally invested in his Kentucky Fried Chicken? Hundreds. How many shots did Michael Jordan miss before winning a championship? How many years did it take before Paulo Coelho's book *The Alchemist* became an International Best-Seller? How many times must a baby get back up before they learn to walk? How many times must you fail in order to succeed?

Of course there is no exact number, but there is an exact answer. As many times as it takes. You see, I know the real reason why people are afraid to fail. They are afraid of embarrassment. They fear disappointment. They don't want to be judged. Some of you are just afraid of the feeling of uncertainty. So what I'm getting at here is that most people are not afraid of anything physical. Not of harm or danger. Not of injury or death. They are afraid of regret. Regretting the entire decision to do something special with their lives and build an Empire that they can be proud of because there is a possibility they might fail. Sounds kind of silly when you think about it huh?

What about the fear of consequence? Isn't that the same as fearing regret and embarrassment? On the contrary, the Fear of Consequence deals with the physical possibilities. Like the fear of being fired. Or the fear of punishment. Maybe the fear of a break up. Possibly the fear of being poor. Sometimes it's the fear of being laughed at. Other times it's the fear of opposition. Even the fear of losing is a consequence we so dreadfully fear. But how can

48

you win if you never play the game? The answer.....you can't. You lose by default. Plenty of people take risks to win the hearts of the person they so much desire; but after the honey moon stage is done and the magic is gone, and all that's left is strife and struggle, those once courageous lovers go into hiding. They stop putting themselves out there. They stop putting their hearts on the line to inspire their lovers to be passionate once again. Why? Because they are now afraid that if they make themselves vulnerable and open to failure, that they might have their hearts crushed by the other. You cannot build the Ultimate Empire with this type of fear.

Succumbing to the fear of what may possibly happen if you attempt progress our business, your relationship, or your health will stop your growth dead in it's tracks. And possibly even worse, instilling that same fear into your employees, partners, children, students, or peers will demolish your success. You cannot achieve success through fear. Maybe temporary success, but even the influence of Hitler was not enough to reign for too long before it was torn down by those with a vision of something positive and loving. Fear can bring you power but it cannot keep it. Respect is forever. It is love for what you do and for who you are. But fear for what negative action you may react with will only create the illusion of respect. For when others finally build up the courage and strength to rebel, they surely will.

Fear is the deadliest and most destructive human emotion on the face of the planet. I now command you to banish it from your psyche and understand it is a liar and a trickster. Do not let fear steal away from you the Ultimate Empire.

Chapter 12
No Doubt

There are plenty of things to be afraid of. There is plenty of reason to fear. But there is absolutely no room for doubt. It has no purpose. There is nothing positive about doubting yourself or your capabilities. But of course, telling someone not to doubt themselves is like telling a married man not to be attracted to other women. He knows that he is to be faithful to his wife, but he can't help where his eyes and mind may wonder. So then, the issue is not how do we get the man to turn off his attraction to other women, but how do we overcome those urges to want to respond to that powerful attraction? In other words, how do we defeat doubt?

Powerful question? It deserves a powerful answer. Let me give you a few of them. Doubt is just fear in disguise as rationality. It is part of your belief system. You doubt yourself in certain situations based on what you believe you are capable of accomplishing. This is calculated in your mind using algorithms derived from the past. So everything you have experienced, seen, and have been told has been collected and analyzed by your subconscious mind spitting out the end result to your conscious mind. Doesn't matter what that information is, all that matters is that we pummel it with new successful information. We do that through a few ways.

1. Understand that who you were yesterday is not who you are today. I mean that in the most literal sense possible. Your cells are forever changing and so is the world. Meaning, even though things may look the same from your perspective, the overall situation as a whole is quite different. People's lives are always changing. Business is always fluctuating. Test scores are always fluctuating. Ecosystems are being transformed. Cells inside of your body are dying and multiplying continuously. So, doubting yourself today because of yesterday is ridiculous. The past no longer matters. Only what you think and do now matters.

2. Best-selling author Eric Thomas said, "Who you are to be you are now becoming." You may have doubts on who you can become, but if you choose to listen to that irrational voice in your head that says you can't do it, then guess what? You will never do it. The universe won't do it for you, and none of your friends will voluntarily build your Empire for you. You have to do it. So, the step you take today will ultimately make you who you are to be tomorrow.

3. "Beware of the thief in the street after your purse. And beware of the thief in your mind after your promise." When legend Jim Rohn said that he was talking about doubt. Beware of this voice. The only way to combat negative thinking is with positive thinking and information. You need to be reading positive books that will uplift you, inform you, and push you to be more. It is imperative that you listen to powerful messages from great leaders and speakers. Go to seminars and listen to successful

figures like Tony Robbins, Brendon Burchard, and Les Brown. Fill up your head with positive body guards who will protect your mind from self-doubting criminals that lurk in your subconscious.

4. Just do it. Nike's slogan. Just do it. The mantra of self-made billionaire A.L. Williams. Just do it and see what can be done. You ever notice the first time you ever do something how nervous you are? You're unsure of yourself and you don't want to do it. But then you get up in sing in front of the church anyway. You write and post that blog anyway. You knock on that door and ask for them to buy anyway. You tell him I love you for the first time anyway. Then the second time you do it, it feels a little easier. So does the third and the fourth. And soon, you've done it so many times that it just becomes second nature to you and that only thing you doubt now is that you won't be successful.

5. I have done two things here. I told you how to think about your journey to greatness and what to do about the mental ninjas that lurk in the shadows of your subconscious. Why? Because you need to understand both things, to not only equip yourself, but to help equip others. What good is it if you have all the confidence in the world in yourself, but your spouse has no confidence in their ability to contribute? How far can a company grow if your managers doubt they can live up to your companies standards? Your team will lose every game if the only confident players are the star athletes. You need everyone in your circle to be confident in themselves. You need to drive doubt out of the office and into the gutter. You need to re-assure

your kids that they are good enough. You have to make your back up believe that they are just as good as the starters. You feel powerful when you're the only non-doubter, but your Empire is crippled by your ego. There is no room for doubt in the Ultimate Empire.

Chapter 13
Invisible Wall

I want to get deep with you now. I wish to jump into your psyche. I ask your permission to climb inside of your mind and present to you what is going on and what has been taking place for years since the very first day of your existence. Am I allowed? Do I have your permission to step inside of your subconscious? Thank you, I am happy to do so. Now, let me show you what has been happening behind the scenes of your own thoughts.

Imagine, if you will, a vast room filled with an enormous amount of nothing. Yep, all you can see is white space. Like a drawing of a stick man on a blank piece of paper, all that surrounds it is blank space. You are now standing on a white floor looking up at a white sky. It is endless and tranquil. This room represents your birth. Everyone is born with a clean slate. No thoughts, no ideas, no judgments, and no beliefs. All there is, is a blank canvas ready to absorb the paint that is soon to be brushed across it. And that is exactly what happens next. BOOOOOOM! An explosion of color and new life comes barreling into your world with no rhyme or reason. Everything is random and everyone is speaking gibberish. Sounds, colors, tastes, smells, and everything that you can possibly experience fills your blank world with astronomical possibilities. Now look around you. The floor is no longer just a white space. It is covered in opportunity. It is covered in choices.

What am I getting at? When we are born, the world is our oyster. We can become anything and everything and all we can see is what we want and need. We can go anywhere and everywhere .There are no barriers. There are no walls. There is only us and our desires. But then suddenly, without our knowing, a new foreign object enters our enormous space. It is a brick. A small brick. Nothing special. It does not talk or move. In fact, we have no idea where it came from. It is so insignificant to our lives that most of us never even see it. It is non-existent to us, so we move past it and continue to play with our possibilities. As time goes by and we go from infant to toddler, this one lonely brick has now turned into a small stack of bricks. Five, ten, maybe even twenty little bricks stacked together to make a little hurdle of some sort. It is not tall enough to block your view of the vast white space filled with endless possibilities. It is not wide enough to keep you from exploring all that there is. It only acts as a random stack of bricks that we may occasionally trip over sometimes if we are not careful, but it poses no threat.

Years go by and we enter into our adolescent stage. Many ideas have come across our minds and many sights have entered into our view. We have witnessed different pains and failures. We have experienced the term no and disappointment. We know fear as well as love. We understand consequences and rewards. We are developing an identity and it is evolving. And so is our stack of bricks. While we were away learning the basic operations of this world, our little brick friends have been multiplying. So much so that they have grown quite tall and wide. Tall enough to block our view and wide enough to act as a barrier. In fact, our once vast land of dreams and visions has now been cut in half by this inconvenient wall. Some of the things that were once available to us are no longer insight. But this is ok. We are not bothered by our new limitations. We barely even notice it. We even kind of like it, it simplifies life a little for us. So we continue to play on with the half allotted to us.

We're in High School now. A lot has changed for us. From our views about the world to what we consider as important to us. We have shifted into groups. A particular clan of folks who most similarly represent us. We tend to either love, hate, look up to, or are embarrassed of our parents. We are coming to a point in time where we have to start deciding what we want to do with the next phase of our lives. Should we go to college, can we afford to, are we smart enough to go, or would it just be better to join the work force straight out of graduation? At this point our mind has developed not only more bricks, but a new wall all together that is connected perpendicularly to the first. Now we have another section of possibilities blocked off from our view. But we have become so accustomed to the first wall that we don't even think twice about the second.

Now we are in college. We have tasted freedom and responsibility. We are finding ourselves and school parties. We are developing into the person we are going to be for the rest our lives. Studying for jobs we may not apply for. Some in University, some in Community College, and others working to save up to possibly go to college. But it's all the same in the subconscious brain. Because in our brains, a new wall has been developing. It is the wall of direction. And with this 3rd wall in place, we now have a direction on where to go. We now are fixed in a tunnel vision like state where we can either stay where we are at, or go down the yellow brick road and see if we like what we see. These walls are a part of us and are necessary for us to function now. We need them as our guide.

56

Soon we have graduated college and stepped out into the so called "real world." We've got our degrees, we do our internships, we get into the entry level and we start paying our own bills. For those who didn't graduate from college, you still have moved out of your parents' house and have established yourself as an independent adult now. Congratulations, you made it! So what happens next? Where do we go from here? Where have all the possibilities and avenues we once used to dream about gone to? What can we envision for the future? Well, for most of us, not much can be seen any more. You see, that once little pile of bricks has turned into 4 massive walls that have now boxed you in. Where you once saw your dream job you see debt. Where you once saw fulfillment you see your kids and spouse. Where you once saw innovation you see obligations. And where you once saw excitement you see judgment from others. You have now been boxed inside of your own mind. Whatever you have accepted as truth for your life is within these four walls. Everything you believe and follow guards any possibility of escape. This is your life now, and it drives you crazy because you can still see the white sky directly above you. That massive canvas, you know it still exists and every once in a while you see streams of vibrant colors fly overhead. Those are streams of hope. Hope that maybe something or someone on the outside might bust you out of this self-made prison.

Typically, as time goes on your children grow up. Your job becomes a second home to you. The weekdays are preparation for the weekend. The only thing to look forward too are holidays and family vacations. You count down the days to retirement as time runs together and the years flip by like pages on a book. Your star gazing becomes less frequent overtime. You look up at the great white sky less and less. You realize there's nothing out there for you. Only confusion and trouble. You belong right here, in the place you know the best. Routine. You become so entranced by the monotonous tasks of everyday life that you don't even notice the bricks forming a lid over you now. Slowly darkening your world until you're completely sealed inside of this mental trap of self-limitation that has captured so many others before you. This brick like prison has been the leading cause of why Empires were never seen. It will be the downfall of the Ultimate Empire you wish to build, for this plague is not limited to only those we consider normal. It infiltrates the psyches of business owners, professional athletes, real estate tycoons, world class chefs, movie stars and life coaches. How? Because these walls are invisible to the physical world, so we never see it for what it is. This is the invisible wall.

Chapter 14
Tear Down Your Limitations

Now that I have revealed to you what has been hiding behind the curtain, it is now time to help you move forward. I must help you to tear down the wall of limitation, for you will never grow into the man or woman you desire to be with it still standing. Your empire will never be built as long as this structure is left unattended too. You must destroy the invisible wall. The question is how?

Have you ever tried to crush a brick with your bear hands? How about chopping one in half with your deadly judo chop? How successful were you? I can already guess that it was a huge failure, if you even tried it at all. But, I think it is safe to say that what I'm asking you is not impossible. I mean, if you think about it, hundreds, if not thousands of individuals prior to this moment have split a brick in two just with the sheer force of their fist. You've seen it on TV and you've seen it on YouTube. It is fact that a human being can even break a cinder block with his head. No doubt about it. Then why can't you? The same reasons I can't. A) You don't know how and B) You're not built for it.

So let's say you're just like the typical person, trapped in this subconscious box, cursed to live the same meaningless life that you have been led to believe is the only truth to your existence. You have forgotten about what once was possible. Every once in a while, someone hints at the possibility of there being more, but when you look around all you see is darkness because in your mind the lid has blocked your view. But now you are on day fourteen of your 90 day challenge. You've been reading faithfully up to this point and something has been switched on. Your not sure what it is, but a click has happened. In fact, the once dark room you were trapped in has been infiltrated by a beam of light coming from the ceiling. It is at this point that you have a flash back. A flash of what you used to see. The dreams you used to have. You become inspired, jacked up, and now you start to feel this feeling of invincibility. Like you can knock this whole structure down in one blow. Without hesitation you go barreling headfirst into the wall knowing that with all of your might you can bust outta there. And then.....POW!

You wake up a couple hours later on the floor in a daze. It seems that brick wall was harder than you thought. Instead of it crashing down, your body took its place. You have been knocked down. You tried to do something different with your life and life hit you, hard. It's telling you, "You don't know what you're doing. You're not built for this." And you know what, it's right. But like the student who has not learned the technique to properly strike and has not yet built up the toughness in his hands necessary to make a meaningful impact, you too must go through rigorous training before you are able to knock down the wall of your own self-limiting beliefs.

You have 90 days to learn how to tear down this

invisible wall. It will require commitment, tenacity, and a whole lot of fight. No family was ever held together by magic, no business was built by elves, and no book was written by talking about it. Rome was not built in a day, and neither will the Ultimate Empire.

Chapter 15
Build You Up

You will not have destroyed that invisible wall at this point if you are just now discovering it. I promise you it's not that easy, though it is simple. But what I want to get across to you is how destroying that limitation will allow you to spread your wings towards greatness. I want to show you what those bricks are really about. I want you understand what allowed Oprah to overcome her lack of TV beauty to become owner of her own show, TV Network and Magazine. I want you to see what can happen if you do what Jim Carey did, by placing a $10 million check in his back pocket and promising himself that he would deposit that check in years' time. I want you to walk knowing how a guy like Lewis Howe's with dyslexia, a football ending sports injury, and stuck living on his sisters couch, has now built one of the most successful podcasts of today and had his first major book, *The School of Greatness,* end up on the New York Times bestsellers list in less than a week of him launching it. Do you want to know he did it?

While you're busy knocking down those bricks one by one, slowly freeing your mind from your own subconscious box, you may begin to notice something odd about those bricks. If you look closely you will see that there is something carved into each one. Words, but what do they say? They say simple things, like can't, I'm afraid, too old, too young, no money, average, impossible, and the list goes on. Is it making sense to you now? Those bricks that have been stacking up against you, deep inside your subconscious, were yourself limiting beliefs. What happened was from early on, you had experiences with certain situations and people that discouraged you. It may have been a family members telling you that you can't be a musician or maybe your first public speech ended in disaster causing you to believe that you were not meant to be a public speaker or even a leader. Or maybe you have seen plenty of success in your life, but for some reason you have developed this inner fear that if you attempt to do better you may lose all that you have gained. So, you never stretch yourself far enough to see what you are really capable of.

For all of us, these self-limiting bricks are harmless in the beginning, but if left unattended for too long you will find yourself enclosed by your own doubts. So now that you know what these bricks truly are, you may now realize that since these beliefs manifested from your own thinking, it must mean that they can be transformed into something else more productive.

Bingo! Now you've got it. It's not just enough to tear down the wall, you must also rebuild your belief system. You must carve out a new message. You must absorb these new positive thoughts so that your energy may grow strong enough to withstand any new limiting thoughts that may and will come your way. You must finish this book in the next 75 days to train your mind on how to think effectively. You must listen to positive messages, audios and videos daily to combat the negative talk coming from other people. You have to make reading your mantra, for a person who reads about leadership can become a great leader. And you must do. Do the things you don't want to do and the things you do, because they will aid in your success. Do them because it is necessary in order to progress. Do them because they're hard and difficulty is the Master of all growth. Do it because it is the right thing to do.

The invisible wall is not separate from you, it is an extension of you. It is yourself blocking your physical world. It is the lid on the jar that keeps the flees from jumping out. And the funny thing is, the lid doesn't really exist, we just believe it does.

When building the Ultimate Empire, you must deal with many different personalities, coming from many different backgrounds and experiences, creating many different limiting beliefs. Your teammates may not believe it's possible to win a national championship. Your sales force may not think they can compete with the top 10% in the company. Your spouse may not believe he's good enough to be your partner in the fight. Not only must you knock down your own walls, but you must help your people to see it for what it really is so they may begin to cleanse themselves of doubt and rebuild a temple of conviction. Get to work.

Chapter 16
Stop Caring About What You Care About

One of the greatest pieces of advice I could ever give you, "stop caring about what you care about." What do I mean? What I'm talking about is your emotions. Those triggers that set off chemical reactions in your body that have you hooked on fear, sadness, or anger. Sometimes it's excitement, peace, or love. It is these emotions that have us jolting off in different directions, keeping us confused, throwing us off balance, and distracting us from what we really came to do. Build the Ultimate Empire. Now listen, and listen well. This is not a chapter on how to do away with your emotions, for that cannot be done. It is impossible to feel joy and never feel sorrow. Why? For one emotion opens up the door to another on the opposite side of the spectrum. This is the Yin and Yang.

This is what I want you to do. I want you to care. I want you to feel the joy that warms your heart when you see your kids walk for the first time. I want you to understand that pain of losing a loved one. I want you to grin from ear to ear knowing that you are the reason you made it to the top in your career. I need you to suffer the responsibility of making sure the bills are paid and elderly parents are taken care of. I want to awaken you to all the things you care enough about to have that strong chemical reaction too. Now I want you to stop caring, and start winning.

Did you know that roughly 100 people die every minute? Not every hour or even every day. I'm talking about every 60 seconds. Every time you blink death strikes again. That is constant throughout the world, and do you think if we as a society stopped to mourn for every person that dies in the world that anything would ever get done? You know the answer. The world is a machine that can't and won't stop pumping. For the sake of the ecosystem, it can't stop.

When Vice President of the United States Joe Biden lost his son did businesses shut down? Did schools let out? Did the military get sent home? Noooo, of course not. Nothing changed. Even Joe Biden went back to work. Every CEO, every Guru, every Top Salesman, every celebrity, and every government official has lost somebody. Everybody has been sick and everyone has been depressed. We all have been angered and disappointed. You know what it feels like to be treated unfairly. But this world does not give one iota about you and your problems or feelings. And when I say world, I don't mean the people, I'm referring to the system. Because we live in a system that if one section of it stops, a whole community of people are affected. Same goes for your success.

It's ok to cry, it's ok to be upset, but you cannot care enough about your feelings to allow them to be your decision makers. You can't let the fact that your boss called you an idiot in front of the entire 1st floor stop you from being a great father to your son. Your son doesn't care what happened at work, he needs his daddy at home.

All the Ultimate Empire cares about is results. What do you bring to the table? How are you contributing to the creation of your dream life? How you feel is irrelevant. If

66

you're feeling good because you just won your first competition of the season and you get complacent, what happens? You don't practice as hard the next week, maybe you don't sleep as much, you probably won't prepare as thoroughly, and it all adds up. Eventually, sooner or later, you get exposed. You become a loser from exhibiting loser habits. Your opponent doesn't care about what you did last week, will you perform this week?

Your husband isn't worried about the great gift you got him last year, what did you get him this year? Customers don't care how proud you are for owning your own business, they just want to know how your products or services are going to benefit them. "Why should I give you my money?" They don't care, so you can't afford to care about it you feel.

"I'm scared nobody will read my book," I don't care. "I'm too tired to write today's chapter," I don't care. "I don't know what to write about," still don't care. "I don't have a publisher," I don't care. "I'm nervous it won't be good," can't start caring now. "I hate writing," I do not, will not, and have not ever cared. I wrote this book anyway because of the ending result I have envisioned. I could care less about the emotions and thoughts that swirl through my head advising me to quit on my dream. But when you're building the Ultimate Empire, you can't afford to listen to your doubts and insecurities. You also can't afford to be blinded by your past success. You should acknowledge your issues and celebrate your victories, but forever keep building on to your success. Understand this for your company, your team, your customers, your partners, and your family. They require a certain result from you in order to be inspired enough to give you their best. Care about what success cares about.

Chapter 17
Believe

I heard the Great, Influential, All-Knowing and All-Powerful, Tony Robins once say, "Find out what successful people believe in and copy that belief system." And you know what, being that Tony charges 7 figures to consult with him 1-on-1 and he is booked 2 years out, I think it is safe to say that he may be on to something.

What do you believe in? Maybe this is the better question, who do you believe in? It's like being on a back to back State Championship Soccer team. Do you know your going to win the next game because you believe in the team? Maybe the coaches? Or how about the achievement itself, do you believe that the other teams will just lie down for you because you are the returning champs? Is it possible that you just believe in yourself enough to lead your team into battle against any opponent because you are at the helm? A seemingly irrelevant question, seeing as how all that we think that matters is that we believe that we are going to win regardless. I beg to differ.

There's an interesting thing about self-belief, it is unwavering. It is biased and loyal to one. It relies on no external forces. The only thing that is of any significance is who carries it, because it is the carrier of this unlimiting self-belief that is considered unbeatable within any arena. Now, of course no one is really unbeatable. No matter how much belief is in your cup, but the one who wields it cannot

68

be held down long, for the WILL to fight again holds strong in this one. This is where we see the difference in your belief system. The self-believer only needs the existence of one self to march forth for they know all the answers they could possibly need or want are available to them at all times. But the individual who places their belief in something outside of self is left vulnerable for there are no defenses left to catch their egos if things should go awry. If you believe in your job security because of the long run of the company's history, then you are left open to the destruction of your income if that company were too fail like so many in the 2008-2009 housing market collapse. If you put all your faith into your star player to carry the team against all odds, then you leave yourself defenseless when an opponent of greater talent and ability steps onto the court like Lebron James and the Cavaliers were when they loss to the Golden State Warriors in the 2015 NBA Championship.

But here's the thing, even though they loss, Lebron has not lost faith in his team solely because he has not lost faith in himself to lead it. Even though many people doubted they could do it the next year, King James himself was not victim to defeat. He held true to his self-belief that he could rally his troops once again and lead a strong campaign for the 2016 NBA Finals. He felt they could win and he was right.

The same with Steve Jobs when he was fired from Apple. His baby, his pride and joy, stripped away from him and still Steve pressed forward with his innovations and constructed a now movie production titan called Pixar. He even reclaimed his rightful place as CEO of Apple in later years. But how was he able to bounce back so strong when his greatest creation ever, which has changed the course of

69

history, was essentially stolen from him including all of his resources and respect? His victory was a byproduct of his conviction in himself. With just that, Jobs knew that as long as he had his mind he could build not only one, but multiple Empires. Only because his belief system said so.

Tony said *copy the beliefs of the successful.* Figure out what makes them tick. That is how you create a winners mind and that is how you build a winning team. Your team won't follow somebody who doubts themselves. Your family won't have faith in someone who is not convinced. Your company will never flourish if they don't believe their leader is up for the challenge. People can only be as strong as their leader is. They will only believe as long as you believe. And if you don't believe enough in yourself, then you will not be able to handle the blows of temporary defeat that come your way. Believe in yourself and that you can build the Ultimate Empire.

Chapter 18
Be Thankful

This is one that I have to constantly remind myself of doing: being thankful. The state of being thankful is a state of gratitude. It allows you to be accepting of what has come your way because you know that you have been fortunate enough to have so many things in your favor. Being thankful for what you have does not mean you have to be satisfied, it means you have all that you need to build the Ultimate Empire. It means you lack nothing. It means that you have the advantage. It means that complaining won't help you, it won't even help you feel better, and instead it will send you down a whirlwind of emotions branching off into a maze of dead ends, obstacles and excuses. This is what you realize when you are thankful. It clears your mind of the clutter and opens up your thoughts to new possibilities. I'm so thankful for the opportunity I have as a free African American and that is why I write this book. I have an opportunity of a lifetime and like my man Eric Thomas said, "You have to take advantage of an opportunity of a lifetime within the lifetime of that opportunity." Otherwise it will be lost forever.

What are you thankful for? This is a very important question to ask. And if you're not sure, ask yourself this. What was I lucky enough to be blessed with that was out of my control? Now this answer varies across the world. We have all been blessed and certainly been cursed in many different areas of our lives. Some more than others. Is it fair? Of course not. But when has life ever been? Is it right? I don't know and we will probably never know. Who are we to judge? What we must do is not judge others, but ourselves. Not compare our circumstances to others, but be aware of the opportunities that present themselves. The stepping stones that dropped next to us. The helping hand that appeared. The wisdom that was shared. The strength we were born with. These are the things we must focus on if we are to be thankful.

Here is a list of questions to ask yourself. To find out exactly why you are thankful. For who and for what.

1) Who are you thankful for?
2) Who has helped you?
3) Who has sheltered you?
4) Who has saved you?
5) Who has taught you?
6) Who has listened to you?
7) Who has shared with you?
8) Who has supported you?
9) Who has been there for you?
10) Who has believed in you?

1) What are you thankful for?
2) What talent were you born with?
3) What chance was given to you?
4) What opportunity was presented to you?
5) What luck came your way?
6) What was given to you for free?
7) What disaster did you escape from?
8) What catastrophe were you spared?
9) What experience haven't you felt?
10) What moment did you not have to witness?

These are just a few of the millions of thought provoking questions you could ask yourself. But the idea is not to answer as many questions as possible, it's to bring peace to your mind and heart by opening up your eyes to things that are truly important. Be thankful that there are people out there willing to give it everything they have just to see you prosper. Be thankful that you have a chance to build something special. And make sure your people know that too. Make sure they know you are thankful for their love and support. Make sure they know that you are thankful for their energy and effort. Be sure they recognize that you are thankful for their skills, gifts, and intellect. Don't just say it, but show it too. Reciprocate and make them feel special. Everybody just wants to feel special. That's how you build special things. That is how you will build the Ultimate Empire.

Chapter 19
Infinite Now

There is no other time than now. Change is the only thing held constant, the now is always changing, and yet it will always be now and that will never change. That being said, let's keep it real. Human beings hardly ever live in the now. We are either stuck in the past or anxious about the future. You are either reminiscing about old times or focused on what might happen tomorrow. Some of us are depressed about yesterday while others are content about what they've done. Many are worried about what the future may bring, yet plenty are excited about what happens next. It seems only the wild animals of the world are capable of living just for today. They seem to have an awareness on what's happening at this present moment. What they are feeling or experiencing currently. Yesterday is over and tomorrow doesn't exist. They can only see the most immediate next step, if that. How peaceful it is to live a life fully in the now.

I'm sorry you've been cursed. Cursed with an advanced animal brain. Cursed with the ability to dig up information from the past that you can use to build a better tomorrow. Cursed with the foresight to see situations happen before they enter into reality, allowing you to adjust yourself beforehand so that you may avoid such a possible negative fate. But I am not here to rag on your misfortune, I am here remind you of your gift. Your gift of the present. Because now is when everything happens. Now is when you will lay that next brick to your Empire. Now is when you will get better and learn more. Now is when you will grow stronger and wiser. Now is when the universe began and your life blossomed. Now is when you will create opportunity and destroy negativity. Now is the only time you will write that book, start that business, train your people, connect with your family, bond with your children, and flourish with your life. When you live in the now, better yet when you live for the now, you follow the principle N.O.W.. No Opportunities Wasted. Thanks ET.

You want to know how to live in the now? You want to know how to limit your anxiety for future events and shelter yourself from past hurts? Just follow the N.O.W. principle. Waste no opportunities. Waste no time on meaningless activities. When I say meaningless, I mean meaningless to you. Don't waste a second on a show that you really have no interest in watching. Stop using up your minutes talking to people about things that don't make you better, happier, or fulfilled. Just stop the madness. Right now you have an opportunity. And that's to finish what you've started. You don't have to finish this book today, but at least you can finish this chapter. At least you cab absorb what has been written. And at least you can apply it to your life for the next level of success you so richly deserve.

The infinite now. Meaning it never ends. Meaning your opportunities are endless. You always have a shot at growing, at enjoying, at building, at sharing, and at becoming more. If you're still living now, you can do something worthwhile. Your family depends on it. Your team depends on it. Your relationships depend on it. If you won't do it now then it will never be done for now is all we have. Remember, your employees are stuck in time. Present them with something to focus on now. Your family dwells on the past. Show them what's in front of them today. Your team is distracted by what comes at the end of the season. Give your maximum attention to the play they are on right now. Build your Empire one brick at a time and one day you will leave a legacy that will last generations.

Chapter 20
Be Happy

Don't worry, be happy. The simplest of phrases in one of the most well-known songs to ever play on this green Earth. It's all any of us ever want to be. Yeah we want shelter, food, and water. Yeah we want freedom, opportunity, and respect. Yes we do all like to have the finest of things. Of course we want to make a difference in other people's lives. These are all common desires. But they all stem from the feeling of happiness. We hope in essence that one, if not all of these things, will bring us happiness. Yet it seems that so many folks are unhappy. I guess it's like they say, happiness comes from within.

To be or not to be happy, is that even a question? I think it is, for I've come to find out that happiness is indeed a choice. It is a choice that comes from within, but not in the vague, mysterious way that we have grown to think. Happiness comes from the decisions that we make every day. These decisions stem from our thoughts inside, but the decision itself does not make us happy. It is the action that follows it. It's when you decide to study for that test instead of watching a late night movie. It's when you take time to clean your bathroom. It's when you spend hours a day writing a book that you have no idea if it's going to go anywhere or not. It's when you choose to talk to that girl you have a crush on. Its decisions that dictate whether we have an opportunity to be happy or not. But our reaction is always influenced by the way we interpret our results.

So what am I saying? I'm saying that if you want to be happy, you must engage in activities that make you happy. To be happy, do things that make you happy. That make your heart warm. That make you proud to say you did that. Participate in activities that excite you, that fulfill you, that make you feel important. Simple.

When I tell you to be happy, I'm telling you to do the things that make you happy deeply, not just on the surface level. Taking advantage of people might make you happy initially, but the heartache of guilt may make you miserable for eons. Eating a McDonalds Quarter Pounder may possibly be something you enjoy on a regular basis, but they usually make you feel like a lard afterwards, and inadequate every time you look at the mirror. Happiness comes from within because choice is an inside job.

Can you really be happy if you make a lot of money but have no friends because you talk to them as if they are inferior? Can you truly be happy if you connect deeply with your family but do not provide enough money to support them? Will you ever be happy if you please your parent's plans for you but never fulfill your ambitions in life of becoming a video game designer? How can a wife be happy if she steps out on her husband because he has spent years neglecting her love language, yet she never told him what she was missing from him? Happiness comes from the ability to choose what feeds our souls, not what pleases the immediate senses. Will you ever achieve happiness if you never succeed in building The Ultimate Empire?

Chapter 21
No Script

Here is where we throw away some of the old thinking. Toss out the cliché's and hone in on what's really important. It's time to get it into gear and build. It's time to throw away the script.

What do I mean by script? I mean the plan, the strategy, the step by step process of what you're going to say, what you're going to do, and when you're going to do it. It's time to improvise. It's time to get moving and get laying down bricks. The Ultimate Empire isn't going to build itself you know? Following what you have scripted in your head that you feel is the perfect set of directions, that you feel is in alignment with you friends and family, that you feel won't bring you too much attention will not magically pop out the Ultimate Empire for you. You have to do what the "geniuses" did. You have to take the leap. There's no script for that.

The smartest thing you can do is not given up on your dreams. The second smartest thing you could do is to start building momentum. Kids exemplify both of these genius traits. For instance, whenever I take my son to Target or Wal-Mart we usually at some point go to the toy section. He has so many toys at home that it would obviously be ridiculous for me to buy him another one. And still, knowing this, my son will spend 15 minutes trying to convince me to buy him a toy. He'll start with the regular "Can I get this toy dad?" I usually reply with a "not this time." Then he might reply with a "Why not?" But it doesn't stop there. Sometimes he'll ask how much is it and if I don't know he will tell me that we should go find out. One time he asked me "Dad, should we buy the play dough or the slinky?" He didn't ask me a yes or no question. He gave me only two options. He is persistent in getting one of those toys. And half the time I end up buying a small toy after saying no to all the big ones. My final rational is, "At least it's one of the cheaper toys." Basically he got me, that boy's a genius.

I have a friend who's a dentist. He told me of how even as a child he has always had this entrepreneurial spirit. He said when he was a kid, he started a tooth pick selling business. He would buy a pack of toothpicks and soak them in liquid cinnamon overnight. The next day he would wrap each individual tooth pick in foil and sell them to kids at school for 25 cents a pop. The kids loved them. They would suck on them throughout the day, and since it wasn't candy the teacher would let them do it. Genius.

What do these two stories have in common? A) They didn't give up on their dreams. My son got his toys and my dentist friend has his own successful practice and a very lucrative publishing company. B) They capitalized on their momentum. Once my son asked the first time, he got that train started. My mind was being filled with endless possibilities of things I could possibly by him. My defenses were wearing down. And the dentist? Well, that toothpick business was just the beginning of his success as a business man. C) There was no script. No long drawn out plan. No five year dream. No list of overcoming objections. No, just their wit, ambition, and desire to get what they want. You know why they didn't need a script? Because they weren't afraid, because fear is irrational. It is something we develop as adults. Fearing things that are of no danger to our health and livelihood.

Now, don't get me wrong, it is very important to draw out a blueprint before you start building a house. That's because it is a very delicate and complicated process that requires many hands that need specific direction. But when you become a parent, you don't have a script to go off of. You just have to be ready to adapt to whatever comes next. When you start a business, all the books in the world are not going to prepare you for some of the challenges that are going to eventually pop up. Husbands have to be ready to deal their wives insecurity. IT techs are going to have to be prepared to run into a new issue with someone's computer. An actor might need to improvise on stage. We all have some sort of plan set up initially, but life doesn't always go along with our plans. What are you going to do when that happens? Natural selection.

Sometimes you have to be ready to take action before you actually are ready to take action. Before you get all the bugs out. Before you work all the details out. Before you read all the books and build all the connections. Sometimes you just have to dive in head first and see what's the worst that can happen. I know what's the best that could happen. You could live your dreams. You could build the Ultimate Empire.

Chapter 22
Resources

Resources, the number 1 thing that everybody who is not successful is lacking. Resources. When I say resources I mean time, money, technology, information, network, connections, skills, talent, support and opportunity. I'm talking about it all. There are so many of you out there who were born with the short end of stick. So many of you who just didn't have enough. The world hasn't given you enough. Your government hasn't supported you enough. Your parents didn't make enough money. Your employees aren't motivated enough. Life is just not enough. And yet people every day go from nothing to something with that same "lack", if not even less than what you have. People have overcame insurmountable odds. People have changed their lives for the better simply because they wanted to bad enough. It's time to start using what you have.

Building the Ultimate Empire does not require the best start up technology with immense capitol. It requires the individual with the best adaptable qualities. *The power of broke* as Daymond John, "The Peoples Shark" and founder of billion dollar company FUBU, puts it. The person who is able to take what they have and use it to their advantage that is the person who overcomes. You do not pray to God for a new hand, you learn to win with the hand you've been dealt.

What do you have currently at your disposal? What are you trying to change and who do you want to become? I'll tell you one thing, we all have access to the Internet. Most of you have smart phones that can link you up to any bit of information you need in the world in just a few seconds. All of us have friends that will support us in a serious situation or when you're serious about what you are trying to accomplish. All of us know somebody or are exposed to an environment where people know other people. Are you talking to those people? Are you treating everyone one as your personal friend? I heard the Sales Guru Grant Cardone once say "treat everybody like a millionaire." Are you treating all of your possible connects like millionaires? Like they have a wad of cash in their pocket and a headful of powerful information?

Your business is lagging, promote more. Your sales are low, talk to more people. Your speeches suck, study speakers on YouTube. You can't connect with your spouse, read the *5 Love Languages*. Your grades are suffering, get a tutor. You don't know how to publish a book, write one first then research the rest after. You can't find Mrs. Right, work on being Mr. Right. You can't motivate your team, bring in somebody who can (email me at motivationalphilosopher@gmail.com for that mental kick in the butt for you team/company).

For every action there is a reaction and for every problem there is a solution. Charles Darwin, English Naturalist in the nineteenth century and famous for The Darwinian Theory, stated that all species of organisms arise and develop through natural selection. Meaning that all organisms thrive or perish based on their ability to adapt to their environment. All businesses succeed or fail through this process. All families stay together or fall apart based on the parent's ability to adapt to the challenges that arise. Your Empire will either rise or fall based on this principle. So how does one adapt?. By finding and utilizing the resources you have in front of you. Find a way out of no way. You have all that you'll ever need right now.

Chapter 23
Audios and Books

The 2 biggest resources I could point you too that will revolutionize your life and help you to build the ultimate Empire are audios and books. I give my audio and book collection all my praise and credit for my success. Some may instead give their GOD the praise. Well, most likely your GOD wrote the very book you live by therefore you can give praise to God's word. Some of you may give credit to the universe. The funny thing about the universe is that everything you know and understand is in it. This book is no less the universe than a bead of water is the ocean. When you give honor to the knowledge and wisdom that comes from these written and voice recorded pieces of genius, you are giving thanks to the universe. Some of you may just want to give credit to yourself. You put in the time, you put in the work. You put in the hours, days, and sometimes years that it takes to create something magical. Not no useless book or silly YouTube video. Not some boring lecture. You did it. I couldn't agree more. I just want you to remember that everything you know now was given to you by someone else who already held that information.

After 6th grade I stopped reading books. If it wasn't necessary for a class I wasn't picking it up. Why? Because it bored me. I couldn't sit still and concentrate on a book. My mind would wonder. I'm not even sure how I made it through High School and College. It was always such a struggle for me to concentrate on reading anything.

But I did end up graduating from the esteemed College of William and Mary with a Bachelors in Economics. A major that required very little reading. It was more numbers, graphs, charts, and concepts about goods and economies. Ironic isn't it, now I have written a book. A pretty lengthy book I may add. And you might have guessed it, I never liked writing either.

Since I've graduated from college, which was about 2 and a half years from this time that I am writing, I have read over 60 books. Interesting isn't it? Before that I started listening to motivational videos my senior year in college. That's what pulled me through my slump when in the first 4 years I worked my butt off, yet I couldn't get the playing time I felt I deserved. That's what gave me the strength to persevere and earn a full ride scholarship for football and win the starting spot as the Tribes leading Running Back my last year, on my very last game, which happened to be the last game of the season.

What made me start to read? I joined an internet marketing company the summer of 2013, just a couple of months after my graduation. One of the major principles that they taught me was the necessity to improve your thinking every day. Me being the extremist that I am, I look that to heart. As much as I didn't like reading, I hated being average that much more. Plus, I was already doing the other habit they advised I should pick up on, which was listening to self-development audio messages. In this case, there was just something about those motivational speakers that I resonated with. Two years later, 40 books down, a mountain of audio messages, and one career switch later, I have taken myself from being a waiter and tree cutter, about to be evicted from my apartment with my little family of 3, all the way to the Top Personal Trainer of American Family Fitness, a Motivational Speaker traveling to speak as well as doing videos all over YouTube, founder of my own Fitness Brand Grip Work Gear LLC, founder of my own non-profit Fourth Quarter Giving, and now author. That's the power of audios and books.

But guess what, here is something I've learned. It's difficult to run a successful Empire if you're the only person growing in it. If you're the only one developing and improving. Why is this? Because nobody likes to get left behind. Not your spouse, not your business partner, not your teammates, not your mentors, not your parents, not anybody. Your company will only grow so big if your leaders aren't progressing. They will slander all that you have built if you are not constantly tuning their mindset, re-motivating them, and polishing their character. That's what these endless amount of books and seminars are capable of doing. This is why I am so adamant about making them apart of your daily routine. Because we all need daily maintenance. Maybe this is the beginning of your self-development career. Let's use these 90 days to start the beginning of a great habit which will end up creating a powerful legacy for those closest to you. Study how to build the Ultimate Empire.

Chapter 24
Write It Down

How do you become successful? Better question, how do you acquire the results you desire most in life? Of course you GRIND. Yes you take action. Sure you must practice every day. Most certainly you have to develop your mind and increase your knowledge. It is obvious that you must improve. But here is another step that the wise ones also advise you do. Write it down.

Write what down? Your goals, ambitions, and your vision for the future. It's been said countless times by thousands, if not millions before me. Yet, it is so seldom done. There's another thing you need to write down too. Your ideas, your to do list, and your agenda. Your plans and strategies should be transcribed; holding everything in your head creates a cluster of thoughts that will confuse and overwhelm you. Causing you too forget assignments, overlook tasks, lose sight of the big picture, forget why you started, and paralyze your movement. That's why I wrote this book, I needed to write it all down to understand completely what it is not only you need, but what I need to be doing as well.

One day I was listening to an audio tape recorded by World Class Speaker Bob Proctor, and in that recording he spoke on a lunch he once had with the father of self-development Earl Nightingale. During that lunch Bob asked Earl a very important question. "Earl, how did you master time management?" The answer that Earl gave has forever revolutionized my thinking and enhanced the productivity of my life. He said, "Master time management? Why, I haven't mastered time management. Time can't be managed. I merely master activities. I take a piece of paper, write down what I need to get done and then I do them." Wow.

What's the important take away from Earl's answer? Two things. First, the obvious answer, time cannot be managed only activities. Second, he writes those activities DOWN. Why? To clear his head of the junk. To get a visual of what he needs to do next. Writing down these daily activities allows you to no longer rely on your memory. You can now focus on one mission at a time because you know that the next one is written down for you to remind yourself. Also, seeing the list in front of you gives you a better perspective on what is most important or time sensitive. The more that's in your head, the more difficult it is to execute tasks efficiently. Remember, your Empire depends on you being effective.

I watched a video on YouTube some time ago with the super successful actor/comedian Jim Carrey. One of his secrets to his success was writing his biggest goal down on a blank check. He wrote on that check a figure that surely seemed unattainable to him at the time. A check written out to himself for ten million dollars. He didn't have much to his name at the time, but 5 years later after writing his self that humungous check, Jim Carrey received a message that he would be earning ten million dollars for one of his biggest movies Dumb and Dumber. Do you believe in what I'm saying now?

I want to be very clear. Writing down your goals

and dreams will not bring you automatic success. Just like talking about getting straight A's won't give you a 4.0. Listing out your activities for the day will not make them completed. You have to physically do the work to make it happen. Writing it down is just a strategy, a very effective strategy I might add, to help clear your mind of the muck of unimportant distractions and help you to maintain focus on where it is you are headed. Here's another great reason why you need to write it down. Because your people need to know where you are headed too. Why? So they will know what they are building with you. "Without a vision the people will parish."

Write it down. And not only you. Your family should have a vision too. The most successful companies have a system written out for what has to be done every day. Championship teams know exactly where they are headed and what they will have to do to get there. It's written down. It's read aloud. It's a reminder of what's to come. It's a guideline of what to do. It's the blueprint to the Ultimate Empire.

They say a goal not written down is just a wish. Write it down.

Chapter 25
Critique

Each of us has 2 critics we must undoubtedly deal with and hear from. The first being other people. The other being yourself. You may call the others haters, jealous, or people who just wish they were you. Some say that critiquing yourself is a sign of self-doubt, fear, and second guessing yourself. Or maybe you're one of those people who take other people's opinions to heart. You become devastated when somebody says something negative about you, what you are doing, or the decisions you have made. Even still, are those who feel like they can do no wrong. That every action they take is the right one. That every word they utter is gold. That they are the epitome of perfection and the rest are just envying wanna-bees who wish they had half their abilities. It's funny. Giving our "Professional Opinions" on matters is something we all participate in, but with varying styles and perspectives. Sometimes we are wrong, other times we are right. Some people we should listen too, while other's advice we should take with a grain of salt. But understand all critiques have their place in this world and some are necessary for our growth.

If you are committed to building the Ultimate Empire, understand that you will attract many critics. Good or bad, people will be around to put their 2 cents in telling you what "you should do." And you know what, most of them will be wrong. How do I know? Because most people will never do it themselves. You see, most individuals are what I like to call "all talk." They talk a good game, give incredible advice, have all of the answers, and yet when you look at their lives you can tell that they are following none of it. Why would you follow the advice of someone like that?

At the same time, there are those few critics who have very constructive advice. Their opinions come from a place of love and not envy. Usually these types of individuals have already experienced the type of success you are searching for. They have already built such an empire. Or they have taken a long, hard look at your situation and have analyzed it in accordance to what you are trying to achieve. How do you know you are listening to one of these types of people? You look at how they live. If you are never willing to trade places and be where they are in life, then most likely they are not the person you want to follow.

But here comes the biggest critic of them all. The one person you have to deal with on a constant basis. Daily is the work put in for you to manage with this person's opinion. They are there in the morning, evening, and all throughout the night. They strike without warning and can become a plague on your life as well as a hindrance to your Empire. Of course, I can only be talking about yourself. You know this and yet many do not know the truth about you. You are your best critic.

Becoming the father I always dreamed of does not stem from what my father taught me. It is directly influenced by who I allow to teach me. I can only progress if I feel that I have not reached a level of perfection. That awareness keeps one on their toes and keeps you

92

consciously on the alert for how you handle the day to day. I must be constantly critiquing myself and so must you for there is no one out there in the big, bold world who understands you more than you.

The ultimate goal to building the Ultimate Empire is making yourself your biggest critic. And that is what the most successful people, in any category, have mastered. The art of critiquing themselves and improving in the areas that they lack. And that is what you will need for your team to do. Sure, you can tell someone what they are doing is wrong or what is it that they could improve on, but that takes time and a sense of omnipresence. You cannot be everywhere and you will not always be around to watch over people in your company, your circle, the locker room, or in your home. You have to sell them on the idea of personal responsibility. And part of that includes analyzing yourself. Wouldn't that be something, to build an Empire that can hold itself accountable?

Chapter 26
Learn it, Use it

This has been a common practice executed by the most successful, influential, wealthy, powerful, and well known people in the world. All the great thinkers have harped on this philosophy for countless centuries. The Gurus of today warn new comers of the following years of disappointment if they choose or fail to follow this necessary strategy; you must learn it. And here's the crucial part. You ready? Here you go. You must then proceed to use it.

Learn what? Use what? Questions that many of you are not asking right now because you already knew where I was going with this. But so many, when you look at their life, are not applying this key Ultimate Empire building strategy. And it usually starts with the first part. The learning.

How will you ever become wealthy if you don't gain the knowledge on how to accumulate and build wealth? Just how? You think you're going to get lucky? Like maybe you will wake up with money stashed underneath your pillow. Maybe you will win the lottery. Quite possibly, you might have a family member die, whom you didn't know about, yet they left their entire fortune in your name. Wouldn't that be awesome? But how would you sustain it? Not sure what I'm talking about? Ok, look at it this way. If you built a billion dollar Company and left it to your child to run it when you passed, but you also decided that they should never have to stress or worry about how the business works because you want them to enjoy the life you never had….what do you think would happen when they took over? They know nothing about the company, the industry, your product, your customer base, the budget, how your assets work, what your liabilities are, what the market is doing, what has made the company successful, where you need improvement, and the list goes on. You left a billion dollar company in the hands of a naive offspring, do you expect much future success for that company? See what I mean?

Ok, ok. Maybe you're one of those self-learning folks. Like, one of those people who spend time everyday absorbing knowledge and educating yourself with all of the latest stats, figures, data, and studies. Maybe you're a Mother-to-be and have read all of the books possible on raising a child. Maybe you're fresh out of Grad school with a brand new MBA waiting to go out onto the streets of Wall Street. Maybe you're a teacher who has been reading books on cars since you were a little boy with dreams of one day opening your own mechanic shop. Maybe you're a fitness enthusiast who loves reading magazines on bodybuilding, health, and fitness with hopes of being a Personal Trainer one day. You have all of the information in your head to do any one of these things, but does it do you any good if you never actually use the knowledge? Will you ever be what you desire to be if you never apply what you've learned? Will you ever know if it works if you don't put it into practice? You won't build anything if you're too scared or preoccupied to lay down the first brick to your Ultimate Empire.

Learn it, use it. Same goes for your team. If you're

teaching your players a new play, you expect them to do it when you call it. How about your kids? Better yet, your spouse. When you show them what it is you like, what it is that makes you happy, you expect them to place that action into their daily routine. Otherwise it would be silly to teach anyone anything, now wouldn't it? So let me teach you this secret. Many folks will not actively search to learn better skills and techniques to improve themselves, so it may be up to you to encourage them to do so. Even worse, many will learn it, and you may possibly teach it to them, but they will not utilize this information due to fear, resentment, or just pure laziness. If they are a part of your Empire, or in the way of you building it, it is up to you to motivate and get them executing their much needed tasks or get rid of them. Learn how to build the Ultimate Empire, then get to work.

Chapter 27
The Minutes

The moments of our lives are composed of the minutes we see them through. Maybe even in the seconds, but it is hard to focus in such small spurts of time. Building the Ultimate Empire is about being a cut above the norm. It's about being above average. And what I have discovered through my countless hours of studying the greats and listening to the gurus, is that the average person is more concerned about the hours they spend doing any one particular action while those who live an amazing life are obsessed with the minutes that compose every hour. Basically, they do not unplug from certain responsibilities in life. They do not ignore the world around them. They do not think deeply and critically only when asked. They think purposefully all the time, trying to make the minutes within the hours count.

A good example is your fellow peers at work. Or maybe even your employees. They usually can't wait to do their hours and be done. Most of them do not game plan how they wish to tackle this day at work. They do not strategize on how they are going to be the most productive. You know when they do it? Day one. Sometimes day 2. Possibly even day 3, depending on the difficulty of the job position. But once they have gotten down the basic requirements, many shut down their critical thinking abilities and just coast through the day because all they have to do is make it through their shift.

Can you see it? How about students in the classroom, bench warmers on a sports team, children at a church sermon, or juveniles doing community service? It's all about floating through the hours so they do not indulge in the drawn out pain of the minutes. It's the idea of someone trying to ignore the tiny parts of time and ride blissfully through, fast forwarding to the good stuff. That's what the average do.

You know what the unique individuals do, who build their lives instead of stumbling into a life accidentally? They make the minutes count. They take the time to put all of their focus into the hourly moments and not just the hours. They pay attention in class to make the grade. They think before committing a life destroying crime. They find ways to make the company they work for more profitable so that their check will become more profitable. They do whatever it takes to make sure they not only get on the field, but they also dominate the Grid Iron. Basically, they take control of their lives.

Living in the minutes is what the great architects of dreams live by. It's this time right now. This hour right now that matters most. Not the series of hours that make up the whole of one experience. I'm talking about the 60 different possible experiences that may happen this hour. This is how you will build your dreams. And if you can get your employees, classmates, teammates, children, spouse, friends and family to live in the minutes at least some of the time with you, you will find life a whole lot more enjoyable. The reason for most Empire Builder's struggle is because of their in-ability to get their team to focus on fighting for the minutes that have been handed to them this hour. You do that by first leading by example. Live in the minutes and build the Ultimate Empire.

Chapter 28
Money=Money

There's an old saying that has been repeated for many decades, possibly centuries. "Time is money." I used to say it too. I mean, it only makes sense right? You put in the time, you get the money. If you clock in, you get a check. That seems to be the base line for how an economy works. Well, I'm here to tell you that this old way of thinking is absolutely true. Your time does equal money. But it is not directly correlated with how much time you spend on the clock. It is in proportion to the amount of value you bring to the market, to the company, to the customer and to your life. And that value is measured in dollars. You see, the value you bring in money equals the amount of money you will receive.

Now, there is also the fact that 2 people could be doing the same exact thing, bring the same amount of value, and yet receive different levels of pay for their services. This has proven to be true on many of occasions for reasons outside of value including racism, sexism, network, experience, education, and sometimes based on what you asked to be paid. But the most common factor is based on you. What do you bring to the table? How do you improve on the system and other people's lives? The amount of value you give to someone will show in the amount of money you earn. Especially if you ask for it.

Time = Time. The amount of hours you put in will reflect on the hours you have left over to do other things. This is fact and common sense. But here's what is not so common. The value that comes with those hours will directly dictate the quality of your hours outside of that task. Meaning, how hard you work will reflect in your pay, your respect, and your notoriety. The attention to detail will reflect in your performance, your response, and you adaptability. What you choose to focus on will reflect in your relationships, your friendships, and how people look at you. Your quality of time is a reflection of how you spend your time.

You can't expect to build the Ultimate Empire if you're spending time doing mediocre things, giving mediocre effort, and having a mediocre focus. Oh no. Money = Money. If you want more money, you have to be more active in money making activities. Whether that be talking to more people, networking, giving better customer service, prospecting, or improving your salesmanship. You have to do more. Love = Love. If you wish to be love, you must give love. If you wish to have a phenomenal relationship, you must be phenomenal yourself. If you want the best team in the state, become the best coach. You want to build the Ultimate Empire for yourself, give the ultimate effort.

Chapter 29
Invest T.M.E.

The most important thing you can do for the development of your Empire is invest in it. This is a matter of fact. Isn't it obvious that you must invest in yourself in order to get what you want? I'm sure many would say yes, and yet this is what people avoid most. They are unwilling to invest in themselves. Invest what? Invest the only things that matter. Time, Money, and Energy.

For anything to be built, created, or destroyed at least one, if not all, of these things must be invested in the completion of such tasks. The universe itself is an energy filled balloon constantly expanding, forming, and changing. Time, is an ever-lasting, completely relative idea that is constantly being invested into productive and wasteful activities. Money does not sleep. It is constantly moving, continuously being exchanged, and always being utilized. So of course your Empire requires time, money, and energy. But how much are you willing to invest?

The world renown author Malcolm Gladwell, stated in his best-selling book *Outliers,* that it takes about 10,000 hours of "deliberate practice" to become world-class in any field. Now, I'm not sure if this is an exact science, but it is a great rule of thumb. If we were to break this down into days we would get 416 days. We are talking 14 months of continuous nonstop hustle, working on the same thing

101

constantly day in and day out. No sleep. So, let's be a little more practical and say you spend 4 hours a day focused on honing your skills, expanding your knowledge, and building your dreams every day. Every weekend, every holiday, every birthday, and every snow day. How much time would it take you to be world class? Approximately 6.8 years. It would take you almost 7 years to become one of the elite, one of the few, one of the best. Meaning, you're going to have to invest a little more than a few hours on the weekend if you want to build the Ultimate Empire.

Money, it makes the world go round. It is what keeps our governments running, our food growing, and our labor building. It is the corruptor of men and beacon of hope. It is everywhere and yet it is totally made up. Money is necessary to begin and to support, and though our dreams do not always require a lot of dollars in the beginning, it can require the few that we barely have. And this is what strikes fear into the hearts of many. Because since money is so hard to come by, so many hours are spent just to earn a few bucks, we as consumers and investors are slow to give away our few dollars if we are not guaranteed instant gratification. We want to see the results of us spending our hard earned cash right now. We can't wait for 7 years for things to unfold. We have a hard time dealing with the reality that it may take 100 self-development books before we are capable of becoming millionaires. That's too much time for possibly no money in return. And yet companies like Primerica have helped thousands of people become financially independent business owners by having them invest a little over $100 of their hard earned money that they did not have to begin with. Phenomenal isn't it?

Energy. As I've said before, the universe is filled with it. In fact, everything that exists now and forever is made up of energy. It is abundant and infinite. But when I talk about energy, I'm speaking on your efforts. It's about your work ethic, your drive, your commitment, your focus, your attention to detail, your enthusiasm, your excitement, your habits, and your belief in yourself. That energy will carry you through any and all adversity. It will increase the value of any dollars you spend. It will bring back any time you have traded. Your energy will convince the world to invest in you, so that you may live in the world you have always dreamed of. Your energy is the glue that keeps everything together when money and time are no longer available. Energy is a choice between you and what you really want. How will you spend it? Or will you even use it at all?

I wonder if your team knows this. Is your family aware of this? It's possible that you are putting in the proper TME and are not seeing the results you hoped for. Your employees don't quite see the benefits. Your friends can't see where this is headed. This is ok. It's not their responsibility to see the end vision in mind. It's completely up to you to show it to them. You must invest in yourself long after those who had your back have left. You must whether the storm until your TME has brought you back a return on your investment. Just give it one more day. And if its still not happening, give it one more, because you always have one more push left in you. Invest in the Ultimate Empire.

Chapter 30
Sleep

There's two different, and yet somehow relatable, ideas when it comes to sleep. We either sleep too much or sleep too little. You either need to be able to push past fatigue, sacrifice sleep for something greater, or make sure that you schedule the proper amount of rest so that you stay healthy and sharp enough to be effective in your work. You see, these ideas have been contradicting themselves since the first talk of success ever came up. And when you dive deeper, you come to find that the action of too much sleep or too little contradicts itself as well.

Look, we all know people who don't get enough sleep and yet they thrive throughout the day. They are effective and they are the most productive. They may not like it, but they need every hour possible to make their dreams come true. On the other end of the lack of sleep spectrum, some of us can't handle going without sleep. Some individuals feel totally dysfunctional when they get less than 8 hours of sleep. And it's not that they are lazy or don't want to work. They just feel they need all of their hours in the night in order to give their best during the day. Here's a good example of contradiction. Eric Thomas, one of the top motivational speakers in the world, has been quoted many times on his philosophy on sleep. "You have to earn the right to sleep." Something along those lines. In one of his most popular inspirational speeches on YouTube ET states, "If you really want to be successful, sometimes

104

you have to stay up three days in a row! Why? Because if you go to sleep you might miss your opportunity to be successful." Interesting don't you think?

But what about Lewis House? The Podcast phenom and best-selling author of *The School of Greatness* has sold thousands of books across the world, has had his podcast downloaded by millions of people, and has built a 7-figure business on LinkedIn. In his book *The School of Greatness*, Lewis talks about the importance of sleep and how it is vital to your success. It not only keeps you focused throughout your day, but is also is the most important factor to the vitality of your health.

The funny thing is, these 2 successful entrepreneurs and public figures are really good friends. And to top it all off, they believe in the importance of how you utilize your sleep every day. Eric speaks on how you must be very deliberate with what time you go to sleep and when you wake up. Lewis preaches and stands by the importance of hustle and the willingness to go above and beyond to get your message out into the world. Meaning they both know that sleep is vital and yet they both agree that the hustle has to push you beyond your pain, fatigue, and lack of time to sleep.

They say money doesn't sleep and neither does the Ultimate Empire. In it there is a constant revolving door. Through it passes ideas, plans, strategies, problems, solutions, help, chaos, negativity, positivity, success and failure. Did I mention that this is constant? Whether your Empire is small or a fortune 500. Whether you are just starting or you are 25 years knee deep in experience. Whether you have messed up too many times to count or have built a life that is to be envied by the masses. Your

Empire is constantly changing, battling and adapting.

You can sleep and miss out on the next opportunity or you can pull an all-nighter and suffer greatly in your performance. As you can see, there is no straight, linear answer that fits all. I think the true answer lies in how bad do you want something and what is necessary for your body to get you there. If you are on the road to trying to become a professional bodybuilder, sleep maybe be essential to your body if you want your muscles to get the best recovery possible as to build your body into peek condition. If you're just starting a new restaurant you may need to go days in a row where you sleep less than 4 hours to make sure that the business is handled correctly on the administrative side, the marketing side, the customer service side, as well as the kitchen side. I don't know what it is for you, but I do know that sleep is very important in terms of how much you need or need to give up depending on your body, your mind, and your current situation or dreams.

Sleep is one of the most important factors to building the Ultimate Empire, so I urge you to figure how much do you need in order to build it right.

Chapter 31
Obsession

CT Fletcher, is one of the strongest men ever to walk on planet Earth. Literally, he has been documented as one of the strongest men ever. In the 90's, CT held the record for the most weight ever lifted in a strict curl competition. But things didn't stay that way for him; in 2005 CT undertook emergency open heart surgery and had actually flat-lined 3 times during the procedure. He is now in his mid-50's, back in the gym, and back to being one of the strongest people in the world again, lifting massive amounts of weight with some of the biggest names in the fitness industry. People from all across the world now come to see and train with him. He even has a YouTube channel that has motivated and inspired millions across the planet. And what is it that makes this once dead man so strong? What is the source of his power, which has allowed him to endure insurmountable odds and push back against father time? What makes CT Fletcher tick? If you were to ask him what is it that make him so dedicated to his craft he would reply, "It is my beautiful obsession."

Obsession. It is an idea or thought that continually preoccupies or intrudes on a person's mind. Some call it a fixation. Some know it as a passion. Many say its an addiction or infatuation. Whatever it is, it is powerful and unstoppable. Based on my studies of greatness and seeing what it takes to build the Ultimate Empire, it is apparent to me that being obsessed is not a bad thing. You just don't want to be obsessed about the wrong thing.

Being addicted to cigarettes is bad for your health. Being fixated on gambling will put you in a financial bind. Being obsessed with watching TV will stagnate your life and ruin any chance of you progressing. Being passionate about helping others will not only change someone else's life, but your life as well will be changed in the process.

Why must you be obsessed with building your Ultimate Empire? Because the obstacles you will face will be many and plenty. They will come at inconvenient times. They will catch you off guard. It will be unfair and unclear why they have entered into your life. You will be challenged at every corner and hit hard at every stop. The problems you will face will be new and confusing to say the least. The people you will run into along the way will disappoint and discourage you. You will lose friends and family along your journey. You will cry and you will hurt. Life will be too much for you to handle. And there will come a time, maybe even multiple times, where you will have to make a decision. Do I keep going on this path or do I throw in the towel? CT could have thrown in the towel and nobody would have questioned him otherwise. In fact, the doctors advised that he do so. But it was his obsession for weight lifting that caused him to get back up and work for what is rightfully his. The Ultimate Empire.

This is your Ultimate Empire and no one's needs to understand your passion for it. You do not have to explain yourself and not everybody will get it. You can talk until you're blue in the face and there will still be people out there who won't understand why you try so hard. It's because you deserve it. It's because your family deserves it. It's because your team deserves it. It's because the world deserves to see your best. But it won't happen if you quit in the process. The obsessed never quit. They keep going until they get exactly what they want and that's exactly what they deserve. Be obsessed with building your Ultimate Empire.

Chapter 32
Be Different

If you look up Arnold Schwarzenegger's "Life's 6 Rules for Success", you will notice a trend in his way of thinking: Trust Yourself, Break Some Rules, Don't Be Afraid To Fail, Ignore The Naysayers, Work Like Hell, and Give Something Back. Do you see it yet? These 6 Rules are his rules, not the worlds and not the average persons. Following these 6 Rules is what made Arnold's life different, because most and almost nobody will follow these rules whether they know them or not. Why? Because being different makes you stand out and feel like you're wrong.

Fortune 500 companies are built on the premise that they were different from their competitors. Apple flourishes and has surpassed Microsoft, who dominated the industry for decades, only because they created something different. So different in fact, that no one has been able to duplicate their products.

You know what motivates a man to ask a woman to marry him? He sees something different about her. You know what allows the woman to give a man a shot at her? She thinks there's something different about him. Even parents are biased when it comes to their kids opportunity to succeed and prosper because they believe their kid is someone special. This is human nature.

Being different is what allows you to succeed in building anything substantial. Being different draws attention. Being different gives you a shot to win. If two NFL teams played exactly the same, no one would ever win. Somebody has to do something just a little bit different to snatch victory from the jaws of average.

Do you think this is the first powerful thinking/self-development book ever written. Hell no. And it won't be the last. Then what is the point of writing it? How could this book possibly benefit anyone? Why would anyone pick it up and read it? I don't know. Maybe the book cover looks interesting. Maybe the title seems intriguing. Maybe the content is new. Maybe the fact that this book has 90 chapters impresses folks. Maybe just the way I market it and explain it or even distribute it. I don't know what it is that is going to catch the readers eye, but I guarantee something about this book will be different and it will cause millions across the world to think and act differently because that is what success requires.

That is what the Ultimate Empire is based on. A different type of structure. A different set up. Something compared to what already has been created. The ultimate family is different in how they spend time together. The ultimate relationship is different in how they communicate. The ultimate team is different in how they operate. The ultimate company is different in how they service. The ultimate song is different in how it touches the listener. The ultimate salesman is different in how he pitches his product. They are just different, but like Arnold Schwarzenegger being different makes you stand out. You look weird and funny. People don't know how to accept you. People may talk bad and criticize you because they don't understand. They don't see what you are building.

They don't know what you are to become. But you know. You understand very well like I do. You are building your Ultimate Empire and it just looks different to the neighbors.

Chapter 33
Patience

They say patience is a virtue. It surely is. But do you know what virtue means? I'm talking about the actual definition, do you know what it means in the dictionary? Virtue is defined as behavior showing high moral standards. It is synonymous with righteousness, integrity, honor, nobility, and respectability. To be virtuous is to show decency. How worthy are you of the Ultimate Empire? Do you deserve success? Have you waited long enough? Better question, have you worked long enough?

Rome was not built in a day and neither was France. This book was written over a period of months with many hours focused on one final outcome, FINISHED. Walmart took decades to get to the top. And I'm not just talking about when the first Wal-Mart city store went up, I'm speaking of when Sam bought his first Ben Franklin variety store in 1945.

Did you know that the civil war happened over 150 years ago? Slavery was abolished and yet it still took another hundred years before the Civil Rights Act was passed outlawing discrimination based on race, color, religion, sex, or national origin. African American Civil Rights leaders like Malcolm X, Martin Luther King Jr, Rosa Parks and Dick Gregory spent many years fighting for equal rights in a time where it seemed impossible to achieve. But they were patient and successful because they held onto a vision. They held on to a dream and now America, as a society, has a chance to reap the benefits from their patience.

Did you know J.K. Rowling was not always a world renowned author, Michael Jackson was not always the King of Pop, Warren Buffet was not always the 4th richest man in the world, and Obama was not always the first black President of these United States? It took time, energy, and patience to get there.

Now listen here, patience does not mean idly waiting for something great to happen in your life. No, that's called quitting. Patience does not mean you wake up every day doing the same monotonous job, following the same average routine, while not actively searching for any new action that may alter the course of your life or success. Spending months in zombie mode waiting to receive instructions on what to do next with your life is not patience. Waiting for your kids to move out of the house to start building your dreams is not patience. Letting your responsibilities tie your hands behind your back and your creative mind lay dormant is not patience. You have a better chance at winning the lottery than waiting for you ship to come in by idle waiting. At least then you would have to take action on buying the ticket that will inevitably pay out to somebody. But these are all forms of laziness, not patience.

Patience is working on a worthy ideal every day for hours, seeing little to no results to prove that what you are doing is making any difference. It's believing in your craft when there is no evidence that you will succeed. It's taking the time on a consistent basis to do the little things right because you know when it counts, the big things will take

114

care of themselves. Patience is the ability to see what most people refuse to see because they are scared of what possible immediate satisfaction they might miss out on. Patience is raising a family based on what you believe to be right. Patience is building a business in a supposedly saturated market. Patience is taking a team from never winning a game to becoming undefeated champions. Patience is a virtue that most people have only reserved for entertainment and not destiny. Patience is diligence and perseverance. The Ultimate Empire is built on patience. Be patient my friends.

Chapter 34
Stay Ready

Let me tell you something you already know. You're not always going to be prepared for what life throws at you. You're not always going to be equipped with the right tools and the necessary information. You are not always going to be on top of things and know when the next punch is coming. You are not always going to see the next challenge. You're not always going to be standing strong. Same goes for your co-workers, employees, spouse, children, siblings, company, partners, teammates, coaches, and every other single human being you have and will ever come into contact with. But let me tell you something that you desperately need know. You might not always be prepared but you should always be ready.

A line I like to use to get me focused for any situation that may arise: "If you stay ready, you won't have to get ready." I say this to people all the time who give excuses why they can't do something. Why they can't attempt that project or start that business. Why they can't speak with their kids or handle their relationship. I especially use it for myself and it always gets me in the proper mindset to combat my next challenge with. Example:

It was my last season as an intercollegiate football player for the William and Mary Tribe. Heading into that season, I was expected to be the starting Tailback. Boy, was I sorely mistaken. My fellow teammate, 2 years younger than me, was put in front of me for the first game. I was devastated. I spent all my life chasing this one dream of being an NFL player and it seemed like in an instant, my dream was snatched from under me. But for some strange and odd reason, I believed I could still earn my spot as the starting Tailback for the Tribe. So what did I do? I GRINDED! I spent 2 days a week, after lifting, working on my footwork and visualizing setting up my opponents for my ultimate breakdown of their defenses. I spent the other 2 days strengthening my neck to withstand hits to the head (I was prone to headaches and neck strains), and building up my hip flexors because they were weak and hindering my ability to break tackles. I came to find that squatting 460lbs does not mean you can break arm tackles effectively. Make a note of that.

Long story short, I won! By the fourth game I had won my position back! And by the end of that game I lost it all again, with a high ankle sprain that put me out for 7 weeks. I missed the entire rest of the season, all except for one game. The last game. I had just about given up on my college career going into that last week. I figured I would be better off not practicing this last week. No running, no rehab, no nothing. Let my ankle heal and then start training for the pros. Then I got the call. It was lunch time on Monday and practice wasn't until 7pm that night. I was heading out of the dining hall about to go lift some weights when my coach called me on my cell.

"What's up coach?" I said. "Hey Mel, I just got finished speaking with Coach Laycock (head coach) and we decided we wanted you to start this week. Are you ready?" That was Coach Barclay, my position coach. After he finished asking me if I was ready, I felt the whole world stop, as if the universe was waiting for me to take the next breathe and give Coach Barclay an answer. As if I had rehearsed this moment over and over again, as if I had been waiting for a moment such as this, I instinctively said, "You got it coach, I'm READY!"

Was I really ready? Was I actually prepared? Not quite, but as soon as I hung up I looked around me and saw nothing my trees, flowers, and a gravel path. I was standing outside in shock. The sun was out, the temp was warm, the air felt just right, and I felt like the world had been placed into the palm of my hands. All I had to do now was grip it tight and it surely would be mines forever. I thought to myself, *this isn't what I was expecting. This isn't what I was preparing myself for, but if you stay ready you won't have to get ready.*

That Saturday ended up being the best game of my college career and we LOST! Haha! Can you believe it? But it taught me something. Achieving greatness requires you to always be ready for the next challenge. More importantly than that, you must always have your people ready for the next challenge, for you cannot build the Ultimate Empire without the ultimate people ready for battle.

Chapter 35
Step Outside of Your Comfort Zone

Tell me, how difficult is it for you to do something that makes you feel uncomfortable? How about when somebody spontaneously asks you to do it? How about when you know you need to do it and the only person around to tell you to get going is you? It can be pretty tough, I know. It's like an obese person joining a new gym. They typically feel highly uncomfortable the first day. So much so that they feel like they do not belong. They begin to feel like the gym is for those people who are "in shape" and their being there is a waste of space and time.

A great relationship requires great communication. All parties need to be upfront and transparent if everyone is hoping to be on the same page. Same goes with a coach and his players or a husband and wife. Communication is key for a flourishing and fruitful relationship to occur. This is obviously not new information and I am sure that this does not surprise you, yet why do so many people lack proper communication? It is because at least one of the parties is not comfortable with expressing themselves, and that is a major problem.

Did you know Blockbuster had the opportunity to apart of the Netflix movie rental experience? They were one of the first in line to dip their fingers into the business.

And you know what they said to the deal? NO! WTF right? I know, I couldn't believe it either. But here was their thinking, they were already so big in the movie rental industry that they felt comfortable with the way things were. They believed that customers actually enjoyed the Blockbuster experience and would rather walk up and down isles scrolling through out dated movies than conveniently order movies and games from the comfort of their homes. This way of doing business, Blockbusters comfortable way, has now put the once dominating industry giant out of business in a matter of months. Do you see where they messed up?

An empire of any sort requires continuous growth and I'm sorry to break it you like this, but growth is uncomfortable. If you want to have a flourishing business you have to do things that make you feel uncomfortable, like sell to people. If you want to have a great relationship with you husband then you have to be willing to communicate exactly what it is you desire from him. If you want to build a championship team, as a coach you must be willing to admit to being wrong sometimes. It might be uncomfortable to admit it, but your players will respect you for it. This is life. The same life we try to explain to our kids or those we deem as ranking below us, and yet we forget to tell ourselves that we have to do things we don't necessarily want to do either if we want certain results.

Having the ultimate Empire is fun, but building one is quite uncomfortable.

Chapter 36
Adjust Our Aim

Building the Ultimate Empire requires a vision of course. You have to see the target in which you are trying to hit. You have to know where it is you want to be. The Ultimate Empire is filled with a set of targets and they are forever moving. Not only are they moving, they are changing and interchanging. The adjustment process is quick, abrupt, and comes without warning sometimes. The questions is, are you ready to adjust your aim?

What do I mean by adjust your aim? Well, in this chapter, I mean a few things. First you must always be prepared to adjust to the winds no matter what your target is. Any business savvy individual would agree. The market is forever changing. The people, though statistically predictable in a general sense, are very unreliable in their decision making and can easily be swayed by outside events. All successful business have a revenue goal for the year, quarterly, monthly and sometimes weekly or daily goals. But how you get there might be different than how you originally planned. You might not have factored in that you would lose a key managing member. You might be blind-sided by a catastrophic event that devastates the country. Your competitor might launch a product that puts extreme pressure on your company. You might lose a huge order during shipment. Your sales force might tremendously underperform due to unforeseen distractions. Who knows what the obstacles or challenges may jump in your way, it really doesn't matter truthfully. What actually matters is how you adapt to it. If you feel a strong wind coming in from the east, can you adjust how you point at your target? If debris is flying across your vision, can you stay focused on the task at hand? If there is a competitor closing in on your target, can you zero in fast enough and make the quick adjustments to clench it? Can you adjust?

You know sometimes the target you are after moves. Yeah, sometimes the thing you want most makes an adjustment of its own. This is most commonly seen in people. Think about the love of your life. The person you have decided to spend the rest of your life with. Even though they are the target in your sight and you have them lined up directly in your sights, is it guaranteed that they will always be in that same spot? In other words, don't people change? If people didn't change so frequently and sometimes drastically, we probably wouldn't have so many failed and troubled relationships. It is because of the constant fluctuation of emotions and ideology that you as the shooter must readjust your aim to keep up with the changing of the targets position.

I recently read the incredible UFC fighter and movie star Ronda Rousey's book *My Fight, Your Fight* and I found most interesting was her ability to dedicate her life to one goal, being a Judo Olympic Gold Medalist. She received a Bronze in the 2008 Olympics but was dissatisfied with that result. But what she realized was that neither Bronze nor Gold would grant her the happiness she so desperately desired. It wasn't that her aim was off, it was that she was just aiming at the wrong target. It was when she shifted her aim to being the first women's UFC fighter ever that she found her true desire fulfilled. Ronda is an example of somebody who not only adjusted her aim but

122

changed her target all together. She went from building an Empire that she thought was for her, to building HER Ultimate Empire.

Building your Ultimate Empire is not about being rich. It's not about being the best in the world. It's not about owning a company or winning a championship. It's about fulfilling the life you desire on all plains. It's about getting the full course meal and not partaking in an entree where you only like some of what's on your plate. It's about controlling what is on the menu. Your menu. And to do that you must have your aim on the right game.

Chapter 37
Self-Mastery

If I could some up in 2 words the purpose of this book, the reason behind all of these chapters, the purpose for why I write, speak, study, teach, and share. The heart behind my motivation. It would have to be these two words right here, SELF-MASTERY.

Out of all the things on Earth I could ever possibly want, this is the most important to me. This is what I hold most dear. Every day I push myself to get closer and closer to self-mastery. Why? For two reasons. 1) I never want anyone to be master over me and 2) only a Master of the self can take hold of everything they truly desire in life. In other words, the Ultimate Empire can only be owned by an individual who has mastered the self.

I don't know of anyone who has completely mastered themselves, but I do know of many who have become Masters in their field. Eric Thomas has mastered the art of speaking, this is why he never gives a bad speech. It is not that he is too good to fail, it is that he is too committed to fail. He has completely dedicated himself to the art of speaking as well as the message itself. He leaves no rock unturned, no book unread, and no peace of advice unconsidered. He is a Master Speaker and like Warren Buffet or John Maxwell, he has completely immersed himself in improving everyday on his craft. Why? Because a true Master has accepted the roll of the forever enrolled

124

student.

Traits of a Master:

  -Always learning
  -Obsessed with improvement
  -Open to all possibilities
  -Lifetime Student
  -Always in a state of flow
  -Top of their class
  -Does not compete, but instead dominates
  -Courageous
  -Risk Taker
  -Best friends with failure
  -Awareness of Self
  -Selfish
  -Has No Secrets

To clarify, these traits can represent a Master within their craft or a Master of Self. The scale on which this Mastery operates depends solely on what you are a Master of. Michael Jordan, a Master of Basketball, may be dominate the game but might only be seen as another competitor in the baseball arena. Leonardo DiCaprio may be very aware of himself while on set, but may be completely unaware of what kind of friend he is outside of the big screen.

But can anyone truly be a Master of Self. No, and that is what makes you a Master. You never stop progressing, learning, and improving. It becomes your life's work, for what else is life but work.

What do you want? What do you desire? What would the Ultimate Empire look like for you? What would it take to have it? What would you have to sacrifice? How many hours would you have to dedicate? What would you need to learn? Where would you have to improve the most? Who would you need to know? What would you need to have? How many days a week would you have to work? Can you do it? Will you do it?

To know self-mastery is to know exactly what you want out of life, why you want it, and do exactly what you know or think is necessary to obtain it. It is to be completely selfish. Now, here the tricky part. Selfishness does not mean unappealing and damaging to others. It simply means to do exactly what it is your heart desires and your mind knows to be true for you. That is how you will build the Ultimate Empire.

Chapter 38
Find Pain

Do you know why a child removes their hand quickly after placing it unsuspectingly on a hot stove? It is because of a natural reaction that occurs from receiving signals from the pain receptors in your hand. You are hardwired to avoid pain, in all forms. Whether it be physical pain, mental stress, or emotional turmoil, we as human beings were created to instinctively avoid any type of pain whatsoever. What am I getting at? That it's not your fault for running away from pain and ultimately dodging your own greatness, because you didn't know the truth. But now you will.

Pain, in the chase for success, is evidence that success is on the way. Now, being in pain because you're getting a tattoo is obviously not an example that success is coming your way, but being in pain because the lactic acid is devouring your biceps from doing 50 curls is definitely evidence that change is happening. So, for the smart- alecks out there, not all pain is good and many of times it is a sign of danger. But typically the pain of perseverance is the most rewarding form of pain you could ever endure.

The proof is in the pudding. Some of the most successful humans beings in the world schedule time in their day to read, to work out, and to go to sleep early so they may wake up even earlier. They typically do this on a daily basis whether they feel like it or not. They do it when

127

they're sick and when they are busy. They do it on birthdays and holidays. They do it when reminded and when no one is there to remind them. They do it when it feels good and even when it sucks badly. They complete their daily routine. Why? Because of the success they receive at the end. They do it because the pain of exercising first thing in the morning gets their day started off with a bang and they are much more productive. They do it because reading keeps their minds stimulated, sharp, ever evolving and ahead of the curve. They do it because having a deliberate set time to get up and lay down allows them to effectively plan and execute their day. Physically they may be tired, mentally they may be drained, emotionally they may not be up for it, but those who have a built an Empire worthy of standing have done it by doing the things that were most painful to do.

Let me fill you in on possibly the biggest pain you will have in building the Ultimate Empire. Motivating other people to do it with you. It's super hard to get yourself to replicate the habits of the obsessively successful, imagine how much more difficult it must be to try and convince another person to commit to the same daily habits when they cannot see a legitimate reason to even try. When they can't see success happening for them. When they can't see why it's worth it. When they think success is GOD given. When they think that an Empire is based on luck. When that other person doesn't even believe in you to begin with. How difficult do you think it would be to persuade others to commit to pain each and every day? Pretty damn hard.

Is it doable? Yes, obviously. I didn't say it was impossible. But when you are able to successfully accomplish gaining the commitment from others on a daily basis, it sure is worth the hassle. You have to see that first

before you will ever get somebody else to understand it.
It's painful building the Ultimate Empire.

Chapter 39
Will Power

What is that? Will Power. I've been trying to figure it out for years. Literally, for years, I've been trying to understand what this "will power" thing really is. Where does it come from? How do you make it? Is it genetic? Why is it so difficult to duplicate? How do you attain it? I've been studying it, mainly because I have been so impressed by my own display of "will power" that I want to know and share with others what it is and tell them where they can get it.

I didn't always recognize that I had amazing will power, more like it's been brought to my attention. A College mate of mind once asked me while I was working as a bouncer at the bar right outside of campus, "Mel, ever since I have known you I have seen you work extremely hard. What drives you?" I heard the same question from one of my teammates on the football team. He was our captain in fact. During our after practice seniors meeting we were trying to figure out how to motivate the team after a bad loss. Our captain asked me, "Mel, what makes you push so hard in practice day in and day out?" I had the same answer for my captain that I had for my classmate. "I don't know, I just want it."

Want what? I want what everybody else wants in life, success. But it has always seemed that unlike most people, I am willing to do whatever it takes to get it for
130

however long it takes.

 I don't know if "Will Power" is something you can brag about, but if it is then I will continue to do it unapologetically because it's hard. It's hard to train early in the morning for years knowing that you will not be rewarded for your efforts today. It's hard to go to class when you don't see a necessity for it in your life. It's hard to work up until 3am when you know you have to get back up at 6am. It's hard to quit a job you hate to pursue a job that might not guarantee adequate returns when you are already a month behind on your rent. It's hard to start a new career path when you have no skill, knowledge or natural ability in that area. It's hard to live your wildest dreams and yet for some reason I think it's worth the risk. I believe it's worth the stress and uncertainty. I feel it's a necessary struggle because I feel success is a necessary achievement.

 What is "Will Power". I don't know. But what I do know is that if you want to build the Ultimate Empire you better muster some up. I'm telling you now, no matter what level or status you are at. No matter how much life experience you have accumulated. Not matter what you have achieved or failed at, the next day will be tough to handle for one of 2 reasons. Either you are discouraged or you are content. Either feeling is deadly to your Empire and must be immediately replaced with hunger. By George, I think I've got it. Hunger is it. Will Power is a representation of your hunger for more.

 Now that we know what "Will Power" is, the idea of being hungry can definitely be captured and created for anyone. Even for your employees. Even your team can be convinced that the only way they will survive is if they win.

Your spouse can be influenced by your own hunger,
creating a hunger that aligns with your goals and ambitions.
The Ultimate Empire is powered by hunger and is built
with WILL POWER.

Chapter 40
One More Step

You know what made Harriet Tubman so great? She was always willing to save one more slave after each one she saved. You know what made J.K. Rowling so successful? She was always willing to write one more page even when nobody had read the last one yet. Do you know what keeps Samuel L. Jackson relevant? He's always willing to do one more movie. It's the idea of taking one more step. I think anyone can take one more step. Like all the times Arnold Schwarzenegger took one more rep, even when his body said it couldn't go anymore. How the Americans fought one more day in the Revolutionary War, even when it seemed like there was no chance of winning. Or maybe how Buster Douglass threw one more punch even when nobody before him had never even been close to beating the legendary Mike Tyson. What could happen if you took one more step?

The number of stories I have read and heard of is ridiculous when it comes to this thing called success. That's really what the Ultimate Empire is, a legacy of success. It is a winner's palace. And it always seems to follow the same story line. A person goes after something they deeply desire. They may get immediate feedback, but it usually takes time. They may see immediate positive results, but it usually blows up in their face. They may reach the top quickly, but it usually is a long and dreadful process. What holds constant in everyone's story, and I mean everyone, is that there always comes at least one point in their lives where they don't think they can go any further. They don't believe they will make it another day. They don't feel they will survive another moment. They are doubtful of the future. Yet, something pushes them to take one more step. To give it one more try. To go one more round. I'm not sure what that particular thing is, but I do know that the final push given in those moments always becomes the turning point in their lives.

Think about all those people out there who have committed suicide because the world was too much for them to handle. Now imagine how their lives could have turned out if they stuck it out one more day. What could have happened? Now, imagine all the folks out there today who have built massive amounts of success and at one time faced the same set of choices. Either to take their own life or give themselves one more go at it. What if Steve Jobs would have quit after his own company fired him? What if Donald Trump surrendered his life after going bankrupt 4 times? What if Beethoven would have given up music after going deaf? How many masterpieces would the world be missing?

You read this chapter, Great, I'm proud of you, now read the next one. Will you? Can you? Are you up to the task? Can you put in another session? Simple question, but for some it will be difficult to answer. For others it will be easy to blow off. So, if you are one of those people who are thinking about blowing it off, who believe another chapter would be a waste of time, who can't see the Ultimate Empire manifesting for themselves, than imagine how the world must feel. Imagine what your spouse may feel when they keep arguing with you because they don't want to live another day not being happy. Imagine how your team may feel because they've lost 9 games in a row and there's only one more left in the season. Imagine how an employee must feel when she hasn't received a raise in 5 years. How difficult is it for somebody to stick it out when they don't see any chance of winning for themselves? I have to keep giving myself a reason to right the next chapter. I have to convince you to read the next one. You have to motivate your team to go one more day with you. To share one more moment with you. To do it one more time.

The Ultimate Empire is built on a series of moments where you convince yourself and others to attempt a shot at greatness one more time. It's always the last time because you never know when your last day is. You never know when your last breath may be. I don't know when I will write my last word. So I write one more time to keep my Empire alive.

Chapter 41
The Secret

I'm going to explain to you the secret to building the Ultimate Empire in this one chapter. Of course you may say, "But then I won't need to read the rest of the book." Logically, I would say yes, but because of what I know to be true it will soon make sense to you why this is not the case. The secret to success, to abundance, to balance, to peace, and to the best life possible is not based on any one strategy. It is utterly and completely based on a formula. A simple mathematical formula that is fixed and cannot be changed in any way. It can be explained differently, but the foundation is still the same. The secret to building the Ultimate Empire lies within the simple formula:

Commitment + Persistence + Focus + Obsession + Vision + Creativity + Consistency + Reading + Listening + Communicating + Learning + Effort + Reflection + Empathy + Work + Positivity + Realism + Dreaming + Studying + Repeating + Goal Setting + Fitness + Nutrition + Self Belief + Risk Taking + Progression + Flexibility + Teaching + Sex + Family + Self Love + Companionship + Mastery + Self Mastery + Control + Understanding + Skill Set + Adaptability + Preparation + Readiness + Legacy + Responsibility + Being Special + Problem Solving.

Seems like a mighty large formula right? I know, and to tell you the truth I could easily due away with half of these concepts because many of them overlap, but I don't want to do you the injustice of trying to tie loose ends together yourself. I want all bases to be covered. I want you to understand fully what success and fulfillment are really about. I want you to know it all so that you may be in control of it all. I need you to know it so that you do not blame me, but instead blame yourself for not building your Ultimate Empire. Let me briefly explain the formula so that you may understand fully how these terms correlate with your success.

Commitment: To be dedicated to a set of daily tasks, monthly goals, yearly resolutions, and lifelong dreams. To give all of yourself completely to the cause. To act accordingly every moment to the manifestation of your desired destiny.

Persistence: Acting in accordance to your tasks, goals and dreams no matter what success or failure may come your way.

Focus: Your undenying attention to the task at hand, directed towards fulfilling your goals and dreams.

Obsession: The thoughts of a particular thing that you most desire dominating your imagination, causing you to act only in correlation with fulfilling your most desired ambitions.

Vision: A mental picture of what you want your life to look like.

Creativity: Original thought and creation comprised of a combination of preconceived ideas put in an order that differs from any other previous notions ever publicly revealed in order to achieve a desired result.

Consistency: The ability to execute a certain set of tasks, actions and/or performances at a previously determined given time, on a regular basis.

Reading: The absorbance of information through literacy for the intention of learning new ideas and concepts in order to improve one's skills and abilities.

Listening: The art of paying attention to another's opinion without interrupting or dominating the conversation.

Communicating: The ability to effectively share information with another so that the other person understands what you are trying to convey.

Learning: Absorbing new information that sticks with you so you are able to recall it later. This new information should allow you to evolve your current actions that will bring your success to another level. Which is why you need to keep reading this book, to learn more new information.

Effort: AKA work ethic. The amount of energy you put into a particular thing to achieve a specific result.

Reflection: Looking back at what you've done. What you have accomplished and failed at. Seeing where you have risen and fallen. Analyzing your past action and results for the future betterment of our decision making.

Empathy: Understanding on an emotional level the feelings and struggles of others.

Work: The GRIND you put in to execute certain actions or attain specific results.

Positivity: Immersing yourself in what the late, great Zig Ziglar would call the good, the clean, and the powerful in order to create mostly good, clean, and powerful results in your life.

Realism: Accepting and acknowledging what is truly realistic. Which is, anything that any human being has ever accomplished is realistic for you to accomplish.

Progression: Growth and upward mobility in any and every endeavor in your life including career, finances, relationships, and friendships.

Flexibility: A physical and mental aspect. Having good mobility within the body as well as have good adaptability to unexpected circumstances, allowing you to still accomplish your goals.

Teaching: The best indicator of whether you have truly learned something or not is if you can teach it to someone else. Teaching is the ability to pass on certain information in a simple way that most anybody can absorb.

Sex: It is taboo to talk about, yet it is essential for not only procreation, but also ultimate pleasure and fulfillment.

Family: A group, a team, a kinship. It is a bond that you share with blood or individuals you consider to be of your blood. It is evidence that you are never truly alone.

Self-Love: It is an unconditional sense of acceptance of yourself, who you are, and what you have been thus far.

Companionship: An intimate relationship with a lover. An intimate relationship with a partner. An intimate relationship with a teammate. It goes beyond just knowing each other or sharing the same space. It steps into being in it together until the end.

Mastery: It is control over your space. It is control over your craft. It is control over your subconscious habits. It is control over you instinctive decisions.

Control: It is acting in accordance with what you believe in. It is following your principles. It is doing what you know is right. It is acting with a purpose and direction.

Understanding: Knowing who you are. Knowing what you are doing and what you are doing it for. Knowing who people are. Knowing what you need to know. Knowing that you don't know what you don't know.

Skill Set: A particular set of abilities or an ability that you've acquired.

Adaptability: The ability to change and shift with your current circumstances and situations in order to best benefit you.

Preparation: Effectively being set to handle and take advantage of the current situation.

Readiness: You may not always be prepared, but you should always be ready. Meaning you are mentally prepared to adapt to any situation that you are familiar with or unfamiliar with.

Legacy: The story you leave behind. The success you leave behind. The belief you leave behind. The resources you leave behind. The network you leave behind. Whatever you leave behind for the next generation to absorb.

Responsibility: We all want some level of authority. A level of adulthood that puts us in charge of our own destiny. We may be overwhelmed at times, but ultimately we want to be able to master it.

Being Special: To be someone unique, refreshing, and new. To do something different than from the masses. To be looked at as different. To feel like we matter. But remember no one is born special, you become special.

Problem Solving: No one is more valuable than a person who specializes in solving problems. It is a skill that eliminated current and sometimes future possible issues. Every company, as well as every person wants somebody who solves their problems. The best orientation is being solution oriented.

I would say this is all you need from here on out, and you know what? I would be right. Yet, based on the secret you would have to keep reading this book in order to stay aligned with the formula. Keep building the Ultimate Empire.

Chapter 42
Follow The Leader

What I have noticed is that essentially people don't like to follow other people if they can avoid it. Now, there are some who will follow another individual blindly if they feel they hold the answers to solve there every problem and need. But, there are also those who would rather continue to struggle and barely make it than agree to listen to the advice of another. Especially that of someone who's famous, well-known or respected. It is a pride thing I suppose. A concept that I do not agree with and have took it upon myself to do just the opposite. I don't follow everything the gurus say, but I do listen.

How do you expect to learn calculus without a professor to teach you the formulas? How do you expect to be a Pastor if there is no one around to educate you on the subject? How will you learn all the ins and outs of football if you don't have a coach to walk you through it? I guess you could just watch it on TV, but you still wouldn't know how to call plays. You don't have to read other books, but you're going to have a lot of trouble formatting what you write if you want to be an author. You don't have to go to law school to pass the bar, but there are many students who finish all of their schooling and still end up failing it. How much of a chance do you have?

The funny thing is, people are more than willing to

follow and learn from experts or teachers of these subjects. Yet when it comes to money, success, family, love, relationships, spirituality, peace of mind, and financial freedom, many folks are reluctant to listen or read on it. It seems that the absence of these subjects in schools makes them taboo to talk and actively learn about verbally from others. People are afraid to be known as the person who created their conscious mind on purpose, instead of by chance like the rest of us. Since when did you start worrying about what other people think?

Nobody likes having a boss, still everybody goes out applying for one. They want to hold a position where they have some respectable level of responsibility, but not too much to where the success of others falls on their shoulders. It's paradoxical the way we think, even I sometimes fall victim to these types of contradictory thoughts, but I refuse to remain a slave to them. I've come to realize that we all desire to be the boss. Whether we are the boss of a company, a team, our household, or just the boss of ourselves. We all desire to be in control and lead. You want to be the leader of your health, wealth, and happiness. You want to be the leader of your accomplishment. And I am sorry to say that most of are just too average and ignorant to do it on our own. That is why it is dire that you learn to follow greatness.

Every day for the past few years I have committed myself to observing, absorbing, and studying the best. Whether it be an incredible athlete like Lionel Messi, a powerful Entrepreneur Billionaire like Sara Blakely, or a relationship expert such as the author of *The Five Love Languages* Gary D. Chapman, I am always placing myself openly at the mercy of their wisdom and knowledge. Why? Because you don't know what you don't know.

143

If you've never built an Empire, how do you expect to build one today just because you decided it was your mission in life? Are you going to just start working or clocking in more hours at work? Are you going to write a book on success or are you going to create a seminar? Do you even know what your Ultimate Empire looks like? How can you lead anyone, including yourself, if you don't know where you're going or even how to get there? The answer, you can't. It doesn't matter what level or status you are at right now, what matters is where you are going, because if you are headed to a new place with new challenges you are going to need a map to follow. A company cannot function without a CEO and a lacrosse team cannot play without its coach. Whether it's a book or a person, you desperately need someone to follow. It may be to push you or to teach you, just know your Empire requires something to be modeled after. It may be one source or thousands of sources, your power source is going to need an outlet to pull energy from. Don't be ashamed to follow, because every great Master was an even better student and every Ultimate Empire was based on a leaders that came before.

Chapter 43
Full Speed Ahead

The story of the tortoise and the hare is very well-known and has been retold and reiterated many times over for generations. Supposedly, to teach some sort of lesson on doing just enough for an extended period of time until eventually you reach the finish line. The turtle moves super slow and the rabbit is exceedingly fast. So fast in fact, the rabbit could easily finish the race between the 2 ten times over before the tortoise could ever finish one. But what happens? The rabbit gets cocky. Takes multiple breaks within the race until eventually he realizes that the super slow turtle has crossed the finish line before him. Basically the turtle stayed consistent in it's process and as the old saying goes, "slow and steady wins the race."

Cute story, terrible message, at least for those few individuals like me and you who desire to build ourselves the Ultimate Empire. How many of us get frustrated when our internet is moving slower than usual? How inconvenient is it when you are on your way to work and you run into a traffic jam? How successful would Usain Bolt be if he jogged the one hundred meter dash? Better question, how many people would pay for Amazon Prime if they guaranteed shipping in 7 days rather than 2? You see what I mean?

In sports, the idea is "speed kills." Meaning the

fastest players will dominate the game. The company to sell its products the fastest will make the most money. The person who acquires their money the quickest will have a chance to retire the earliest. The rate at which you complete things is crucial not only to your success, but even to your survival.

Cancer patients don't have time to play the steady game. Every minute is crucial to win the battle for their life. They can't afford to take their treatment nice, slow and steady. They've got to hit it full force and dominate the playing field, which is their own body.

If you want to be average, fine. Moving steadily within the pack will allow you to save just enough energy that you don't feel overwhelmed, fatigued, and beaten down. A steady pace will allow most people to at least finish the race. Slow and steady can get you to the finish line in a lot of things, but not in success and definitely not in building the Ultimate Empire. Why? Because there is a time limit on everything. You only have so many hours to complete a project, so many minutes to connect with a customer, so many seconds to share with your lover, so little time to do great things and yet most people act like they have forever. As if they know when their time will be up. As if there is no competition. Like nobody out there could possibly take their girl, that's why you haven't proposed to your girlfriend after ten years of dating. Yet, so many women have left a relationship because their would-be husband took too long.

Being steady will definitely get you to the finish line, but you have to be fast if you want to win at anything. If you think about it, that's what the Ultimate Empire is, a victory. Whether its sports, spouse, college, job, promotion,

146

business, stocks, investments, retirement, house, cars, board games, or even the lottery. It's always about how did you fair. Even your own piece of mind goes up on the board as either a win for you today or a failure. And you can't win being slow, no matter how steady you are because there are those individuals, many of them in fact, who have built up the WILL to run the race fast and keep it steady until the end. Those are the ones who get most of what they want in life. From the general stuff down to the smallest details. Time is always ticking against you, someone is always working for what you want, you better move fast and kill any chance failing. God speed.

Chapter 44
Stop Trying

"I'm getting ready, to start thinking about, doing it, one day." Sound familiar? That excuse someone gives you when you ask them when they are going to start doing something. Maybe it's your son after you've asked him when he is going to clean his room. Maybe it's your wife when you ask her when she is going quit smoking. Maybe it's your friend after you ask when they are going to start going to the gym with you. Maybe someone just asked you when you're going to start that business? When are you going to finish that book? When are you going to study? When are you going to look for a job? When are you going to watch those videos? When are you going to turn your life around? Just when exactly? A question we all have to answer at some point.

It's hard to hold ourselves accountable. Probably because there is no one better at persuading why we are not ready to do something than ourselves. When it comes to procrastination, we can easily can come up with a million excuses why we can't or haven't done it. I need to make more money, I need to consult with someone first, I need a better idea, I need to see how the economy does, I need to see who becomes President, I'm waiting for the timing to be right, I'm looking for a partner, things aren't that bad yet, I want to see how things play out, let me try it my way first, after the baby is born, and all that jazz. With a laundry

148

list of excuses, how does anything get done? It gets done because of 2 reasons. Necessity and desire.

Stop trying. Stop trying to make things happen and just make them happen. Stop trying to do better. Stop trying to get started. Stop trying to change. Change. Do better. Get started. Make it happen. Go do it. Do what's necessary. If you need a job, you will do what is necessary to get a job pronto if it means keeping your family from being kicked out on the streets. If you desire to go to college, you will go to whatever community college, work whatever job, and apply for every scholarship imaginable in order to guarantee yourself the opportunity to earn a higher education. Desire is what created America. Necessity is what freed the slaves. The need for a better life is what pulls individuals out of poverty. A deep burn for change is what put an African American into the White House. Obama didn't talk about doing it one day, he did it, TWICE!

Many people will try to read this book. They will even try to open it up and fail to do that much. CEO's will try to turn a company around. Coaches will try to listen to their players. Teachers will try to connect with their students. Police Officers will try to be more patient with citizens. Plenty of people will try, but few will do. And I don't mean that those few will never fail. I mean they will go into a thing with the full intent of making their hopes and wishes a reality and if they fail today, they will fight again with the same intent to make it happen tomorrow. The Ultimate Empire you wish to build, whether you are a millionaire or a non-profit employee; It will never stand tall and strong, it will never be fully constructed, and it will never see the light of day if you spend the rest of your life *trying* to do more. *Trying* to be more. Being rich doesn't make you accomplished. Neither does being married and raising a family. Building something that is timeless, fulfilling, and is the full expression of you. That is an accomplishment. Now do something.

Chapter 45
Don't Quit

Trials and tribulations are expected. Not only when you are building the Ultimate Empire, but also during your entire existence. It is inevitable. You will be tried and you will be challenged. You can run and you can try to hide but it will not do you much good. You know that, I know that, your team and your family knows that. Even children know that, and yet we are still prepared to quit when things get too tough for us. Why is that?

The irony that when I receive a new client for me to whip into shape and they tell me how they are geared up and ready for me to kick their butt. How they don't what me to hold back. How they are ready to essentially die for the cause. They want to get back into shape and they want it bad, so they have come to me to torture their fat cells and improve their muscle capacity. And then when the pain begins almost the same reaction is always expressed. They don't feel well and they are not sure if this is really for them.

Do you see the problem here? It is that pain that distracts us. It is a natural reaction and is to be expected. Wherever there is some sort of pain or discomfort, the brain automatically forms the conclusion that we must retreat and flee from whatever is the root of this unfortunate happenstance. It is natural, but like you and I know, it

151

doesn't mean that it's right.

The real issue is not you. It is not your group's lack of mental toughness. It is not your resolve. It is not your weakness. It is not even the source of pain itself. It is your understanding for doing what you are doing. This is what separates the back-to-back championship teams from the pack. This is what creates fortune 500 companies from used to be struggling start-ups. This is what creates Instagram Models out of the average gym goer. It is one's deep and continuous understanding of why? Why go through it? Why push past it? Why continue? Why is it important? Why is it necessary? Why is it powerful? Just why, we need to know why!

Allot of times, telling children they can't do something just because we said so is not enough reasoning to make them not to give it a try, despite our fair warning. It is because the reasoning for not doing so is not deep enough. They may understand your words, but if you do not effectively communicate that WHY to them, then your threatening remarks will fall off deaf ears, resulting in complete disregard of your instructions. To not fully explain, inform, and engage in your fellow team member or even family is to quit. You are quitting on them. You are quitting on your leadership role. You are a quitter and a quitter will only produce more quitters.

There will be many days, an uncountable amount of days, when you will want to quit. Maybe your job, maybe your relationship, possibly a book you are writing or reading. But what will be your benefit for doing so? Is it really worth giving up on? If it is, then by all means do, but if it's not then keep going. See here, I'm giving you a reason, possibly a deeper reasoning to not give up on building your Ultimate Empire. But it doesn't stop there, every chapter is meant to do the same. Do you get it? Every day you must find new information to hold on to that will allow you to press forward through the most difficult of times. You need to drown out the loud screeching noise of pain and ignore the mega phone voice telling you to pack it in. The only way to do that is to find a reason to keep going. I'm telling you not to quit on your goals and dreams for the same reason you're telling your family to keep believing in you. Because it's worth it.

Chapter46
Repetition

I talked about this in a speech earlier today before writing this chapter. The importance of repetition. They say repetition is the Father of all learning and the Mother of all skill. Some call it practice, while others know it as drilling. It is a process that is replayed over and over again. It is a set of movements that are being copied and re-copied. It's like putting your favorite song on repeat. Every time you hear it again it's like you gain a deeper understanding of the music. That's how it is for the athlete. That's how the pianist plays so elegantly, as if her fingers and the keys have merged into one cord. That is how the student becomes Valedictorian. It's all due to the habitual repetition of certain actions and thoughts.

Kobe Bryant is arguably one of the greatest NBA players to have ever played the game. I believe rightfully so. It would be easy to say that he had God given talent and that anyone blessed with the height of being 6'6" could play at such a level. If only such ignorance were true, but I think the professional league would be a lot more even across the board in their winning percentage. I once heard about the ridiculous practice regiment that Kobe often did. He would spend hours late at night, up through the morning shooting shot after shot. In fact, a coach from one of the Olympic Teams that Kobe was a part of gave his account one time. He explained how Kobe had called him at 4am to help him with some conditioning. The coach agreed, but being his first time working with the Lakers All-Star he was not quite sure about what he was getting into. For 2 hours he had Kobe doing condition drills and lifting weight. By the time they were done his coach was exhausted and Kobe was ready to shoot some baskets. The coach hit the sack to rest a few hours before the team's 11am practice. When he returns, he and the other players find Kobe up early shooting some more practice shots, perfecting his game. Thinking he just gotten there himself, the coach asks Kobe, "When did you finish?" Kobe responded, "I wanted to make 800 shots, so I just finished now."

Now, this isn't word for word, but it is an actual account given of an individual's dedication to constant repetition. And what does he have to show for it? 5-time NBA champion, 2-time NBA scoring champ, League MVP, Finals MVP, All-Star MVP, 18-time NBA All-Star, as well as NBA Slam Dunk Contest Winner. You've got to be more than just tall to do that.

A business is built on doing the right set of actions repeatedly every day. Not just on Mondays. Not just on the weekdays. Every single day. McDonalds cooks its world famous fries the same way, every day, and at every location. Why? Because they understand the power of repetition. It's duplicable. It's clear. It's simple. And they understand the more you do a thing, the better at it you will become.

I read every day, repetition. So does Warren Buffet. 6 hours a day to be exact. CEO's of big multi-billion dollar companies tend to follow the same routine almost every day. They get up at the same time, they workout at the same time, they read emails and eat breakfast at the same time. They may even eat the same food every day. They repeat their routine over and over trying to do it as good as or even better than they did it the day before. Why? Because we can always do better. You can be a better mother or father. You can become a better leader and listener. You repeat to improve. To make certain actions second nature, so when faced with adversity or opportunities you are quick to adapt and claim your victory.

It's difficult to stick to a routine. Even though the Ultimate Empire requires it, people tend to get bored and distracted. Life itself is distracting. Especially in this day in age. The world is moving at the speed of microprocessors and time is money. It is not slowing down for anyone. Technology is evolving, economies are changing, wealth is shifting, and information is being transferred at light speeds. This is why, now more than ever, the ability to repeat foundational actions is extremely important if you ever want to create a successful career, happy family and your Ultimate Empire.

Chapter 47
Don't Repeat In Vain

Now that we've gotten the cliché out of the way, it's time to understand where most people lack in. The ability to repeat intelligently, productively, and not in vain.

Once there was a boy. He grew up in a nice suburban home with both parents who both had good jobs. He had a pretty happy childhood, had exciting holidays and always got what he wanted. And the food, oh don't get me started. It was to die for. Mom could certainly throw down in the kitchen. Dad, not so much, but he tried. The little boy had a pretty awesome childhood until one day while in school, he gets called down to the principal's office. Not sure what's happening, the little boy heads over. As he approaches the office he can see his mother in the hallway, crying. It was obvious at this point that something was wrong, very wrong.

Come to find out, the little boy's father had surprisingly had a heart attack and died on the way to the hospital. What makes it not so surprising is that the boy's father had some health issues. He had high cholesterol and high blood pressure. He was overweight and borderline diabetic. He worked out occasionally, but nothing to strenuous. He drank around 2 or 3 beers a night after work each day and only had coffee for breakfast, takeout for lunch (if he remembered to eat lunch), and a big hardy meal for dinner. He was a heart attack waiting to happen. He knew these things of course. His doctor prescribed him medication for his irregular test results and advised him to go on a diet, as well as cut down the drinking. But the boy's father would just reply cheerfully. "Don't worry doc, I'm strong as an Ox. These things just run in my genes. And you know what? My dad has lived the same way for years and is still alive today." I guess life span isn't hereditary.

This is the story of a lot of people. We tend to eat the way our parents ate and ignore the many side effects that try to alert to us that we are doing the wrong thing. This is ignorant repetition.

They say doing the same thing over and over again expecting a different result is the definition of insanity. This has definitely been proven in the Sales world. Many individuals who work for big time insurance agencies or time share resorts, or even real estate agencies, fall into this category. There is a reason why only a select few are successful in the world of sales. It is because they repeat what the other successful people are doing and not what the masses of "normal" people are doing. Most people are so desperate to fit in and live comfortably that they lock themselves into a box of mediocrity. Then when they receive mediocre results they can't seem to understand why. They are repeating what everybody else is doing, so why aren't they at the top of the results? They are merely copying unproductive strategies and no matter how well you master them, you will only become the master of average pay.

This is a crucial of practice you should implement immediately, to never repeat in vain. And also don't repeat success part time. Meaning, don't start practicing on your game, parenting, reading, writing, studying, communication, fitness, and create awesome results just to stop halfway. In fact, you should never stop. These intelligent, productive, and successful practices should be adopted for life. Why not? You're only going to live for as long as you are breathing, why not make every breath worth taking? Why not make everyday a step in a better direction? Why not make a little more money today, make a few more connections today, and give your family a few more smiles? Why not be the change instead of complaining about the need for change? When you repeat successful habits, make sure you make a vow to repeat them for life.

The foundation to your Ultimate Empire is your most practiced habits. What you do every day. What your family does every day. What your team does every day. What your staff does every day. If it's built on repetition. It's built on discipline. Do not get this far in your 90 day reading challenge and fall off. Or start to miss a day here and there. Repeat the exercise each and every day until you have finished. Until the transformation is complete. "You've come too far just to come this far" said Eric Thomas. Now finish the race.

Chapter 48
Work Ethic

Might as well call it Repetition part 3. Doesn't most work involve some form of repetition? That would make a hard worker someone who is committed to the art. But the reason why I have broken this down into a separate chapter is because I want you to understand what work ethic is.

Ethics, according to Google, is a set of moral principles. Work ethic is the principle itself, that hard work is intrinsically virtuous or worthy of reward. Here, we understand that work ethic is not a verb, it is a belief. A person who is always looking for the easy way out is who we would label as having a low work ethic. A person who works hard for a very labor intensive industry does not necessarily have a high work ethic. Work ethic is measured by your daily efforts. It is still measured by your goals and desires, as well as how your actions align with them. Your work ethic is your religion. And whatever you most believe in you will certainly follow. If you believe that you can become a billionaire and that is a priority for you, you will undoubtedly have a high enough work ethic to accomplish just that. But it has to be those two things combined. You have to believe first you can do it, and second it must be a priority. Meaning it's the first thing on your list every day and you think in critical/creative terms in order to gain one step closer to your dreams.

160

Mark Minard, Owner and Founder of the a facility built for adults with special needs called Dreamshine, is the definition of what it means to have a high work ethic. First off, to create a successful business from scratch requires incredible belief in one's self and it would have to be your almost highest possible priority in life. Probably second only to breathing. Why? Because the competition is endless in business. Whether it's a non-profit or a for-profit, it is still considered a business and people still need to make money. Investors are involved, your opponents don't want to see you succeed, and you are uncertain everyday of your life on what you are doing. Starting your first business is like telling someone to climb a mountain without any formal training on the proper rock climbing techniques and strategies. And that's exactly what Solid Dude, AKA Mark Minard did as he explained in his book *The Story of You*. He got to climbing.

Mark saw that there was a need for high quality care and services for adults with special needs that the current administrations were just not providing. He felt like it was his duty and obligation to create a program that gave these types of individuals a place to grow intellectually, skillfully and socially. Mark felt they needed more than just a baby sitter, they needed a community and after months of studying, certifying, rejections and threats, he and his sister Amy Minard were able to establish Dreamshine. After ten years it still stands.

How do you overcome adversity? You work through it. How do you defeat challenges? You out work failure. But this is pretty much a given. You and I both know this without a doubt. Then why doesn't everybody including your team know it? Is it because they don't like hard work? No, it is because their success religion is different from yours. They don't believe they can win no matter how hard they work. Or success is not a priority to them. Or they feel that committed work in this is a waste of time. You have to change their work ethic. You have to change their success religion.

You can believe in yourself that you can build the Ultimate Empire all you like. You can even make it your everyday most important agenda. But all Empires need people and if those people do not have the same work ethic then your Empire will never rise and whatever you build in hopes will eventually crumble. Create a religion of high work ethic.

Chapter 49
Defeat pain

The only material strong enough to transform you into a success is pain. Notice I did not say create success. Success in anything can manifest by sheer luck and circumstances. In order to turn yourself into a successful person, meaning to create the life you desire in all aspects, you must physically, mentally, and emotionally travel through pain. Not only that, but you must also defeat it.

Building a brick house by hand is painful on the body. It is tedious for the mind and can make you feel discouraged at times. This is why we do not build houses by hand anymore, but that is how we build the Ultimate Empire. Brick by brick, day by day. Whether we are working on our fitness, diet, business, degree, diploma, love life, family or even writing a book, we must go through this pain. Though this is not a shocker to most, many of us try to avoid this pain at all cost. As if we ever really could. You can try watching the news or scrolling through Facebook and other Social Medias to try and distract yourself from the impending doom, but eventually life will catch up with you and you will be forced to pay the piper. You can try building a smaller, less complex home for yourself to save yourself time on labor. You can use cheaper material and ignore coaching. You can take shortcuts and leave out screws because there were a few missing in the package. Yes, the grind will be over alot sooner, but the backlash will also be a lot greater. The maintenance will be more frequent, your ability to find the actual problem will be hindered, and your safe haven will be ill-equipped to handle the many storms that will pass through your neighborhood. I don't even want to imagine when a natural disaster strikes.

What does it mean to defeat pain? It means you do the activities that are uncomfortable for you to some degree. You do them when it hurts, when it's boring and when it's embarrassing. And you keep doing it until you win. You don't stop when it becomes too much to handle. You outlast it. You endure it. You press forward. You deal with it and you improve upon. Why? That's how wars are won.

We know what it means to go through physical pain. Like when you go to work with a stomach ache because you know that unless you are dying your boss expects you to be at the office. Like when you go to cheerleading practice with a bruised ankle because the big State Competition is next week and your team needs you to be ready. Physical pain is a common experience in our lives. But we tend to only go through it when we feel we have to. Which is natural because our bodies pain receptors are meant to warn us from things that are possibly dangerous to our health and wellbeing. They asked one of the greatest boxers of all time, Muhammad Ali, how many sit ups he did every day. "I don't count my sit ups. I only start counting when it starts hurting because that is when it really counts" was his response.

Mental pain is what human beings are notorious for avoiding and television has exploited that. Why do you think so many people claim to be "not good at math?"

164

Because it requires the most brain power. You can't answer any mathematical question based on life experience. You have to know the exact formula. You have to do some real studying. And it's not like we use these formulas in everyday life so math is almost a foreign language to us. The same reason why most people know very little if anything about their finances. It's foreign. It requires great brain power and energy. The answer isn't obvious. But for those ten million or so people who have taken it upon themselves to learn how money works, they have become Americas current millionaires in the 21st century.

Emotional pain is the toughest and most unexplainable pain that we deal with. We don't understand it, we can't see, and we don't know why it's happening half the time. Emotional pain is stupid. But it is also very real and affects us all very deeply. Because it cannot be seen, people tend to ignore its validity. We try to ignore it. We frown upon others going through it. We pretend we don't need help. We act like it will just go away on its own and most likely it will. But this form of dealing with pain does not create new growth in our wisdom, only new clutter in our attic. Joe Biden lost his only begotten son while serving as Vice President of the United States. It was an incredible blow to his life, his wife, and his family. He could have easily step down from his position as Vice President and nobody would have questioned him. He could have taken the easy way out and let the pain of lost consume him. But instead he persevered. I've never spoken with Biden myself, but I would guess it was because he understands that unfortunate things happen to people in every country of the world every day and his situation is nothing special. Continuing to serve and lead is the only thing worth living for, not mourning for all of eternity.

Pain is unshakeable and is headed your way right now. You and I know this, but does your family know this? Do your kids know this? It would be wise to equip them with the mental tools to combat that pain. It would be wise to persuade your team why they should push through that pain. It would be beneficial if you were to prepare your students to overcome that pain. It would be in your best interest to finish what you started. Building the Ultimate Empire.

Chapter 50
You Succ

Thomas Edison and Albert Einstein. Some of the most highly regarded and widely respected scholars in human history. Did you know that they were once considered unteachable in grade school? John C. Maxwell. Considered the world's top expert on leadership and has written over 60 books. Did you know that he struggled in leading his congregation in the beginning years of being a lead pastor of his church? Oprah Winfrey. Possibly the most powerful woman in television. Did you know that she was fired from her first TV job as a news anchor because they claimed she was cosmetically challenged. Chris Gardner. He is owner and founder of Gardner Rich & Co, a stock brokerage firm. Did you know that before becoming a multimillionaire, Gardner was living homeless with his adolescent son after the divorce of his former wife? Did you know that I've almost been evicted twice from my apartment with me, my girlfriend, and our son?

Success is a funny word. When we think success we usually associate it with a winner. Someone who is rewarded generously. Someone who is on top of their game. No one ever thinks of success as being bad at something. But if you've noticed, when you read the stories of the most successful individuals in the world it is almost across the board the same. They all "succed" at some point.

The mind is well known for confusing us and writing up it's own stories on how other people's lives have unfolded to where they are now. People's success is no different. We get caught up in the glamour and forget that they are human beings. And all human beings must go through a period of immense suckage before they can ever expect to build the Ultimate Empire. Success begins with "Succ". You have to suck at it first. Doesn't mean you can't be talented, just means you won't be considered one of the best until you are first humbled and forced to hone your skills to an elite level. It is "ESS-ential."

I think you get it now. They've been saying it for generations now. Success leaves clues. Not just the successful individuals who have reaped the generosity that being successful gives, but from the word itself. It is telling you that it is ESSential to SUCC at something first before you become truly Succ-Essful. Being that success is a journey and not a destination, you will find that you SUCC at many things the first time.

This is where the disconnect takes place. From leaders to subordinates. From teachers to students. From Masters to beginners. From professionals to amateurs. From the architect to the builders. Even from the parent to the child. There is a misconception and a misunderstanding. Too many people are misled to think that it's pure talent that will get you to the top. That it takes some God given abilities to be good enough. That success can't be taught, you must be born into it. Fredrick Douglass proved that theory wrong. Napoleon Hill proved it wrong too. Helen Keller is ultimate proof. She was blind and deaf and still was successful, but people forget that. Sometimes you may forget that too. That's why we must be reminded again that it is ESSential to SUCC first, but if you persevere you will build the Ultimate Empire.

Chapter 51
Meditation

If you're a reading this book one chapter per day I would like to say congratulations for making it to day 51. Notice, these chapters are not meant to give you the meaning to life or even the keys to success. *90: Building the Ultimate Empire* is a weapon. A weapon against mediocrity, negativity, doubt, fear, and hopelessness. It is your attempt to understand people's mental hurdles as well as your own. To understand how thoughts work. It is a distraction from distractions that would ultimately be the source of your demise. It is a wakeup call. It is a strategic war plan and its purpose is to ensnare your negative beliefs and set free your imagination. This is the next step in your understanding so that you may be transformed and help others do the same. Though many will resist your attempts and wisdom, you will have had a deep understanding why, even though what you preach is obviously true. This is Batman's utility belt. With it you know what to reach for when in trouble.

Now I want you to meditate on that. What do I mean by meditation? I mean think deeply and honestly. Think wildly and carefree. Think irrationally and think realistically. Think selfishly and caringly. Just think and do it alone. Maybe in your room. Maybe in the kitchen. Maybe sitting crisscross apple sauce with your eyes closed and your hands in prayer formation while Tibetan chants are being played in the background. Me personally, I enjoy my quiet time in the shower. I think it has something to do with the water. It allows my thoughts of flow so-to-speak. I get into a thinking rhythm. Maybe it will do the same for you. But no matter where you do it, or how you do it, just try it. What for? To be still your life.

Your life is moving fast and in a hurry. How do I know? Because my life is doing the same. Don't worry, it is normal. Too normal. We miss things because of it. We miss what's important. You get so caught up in building the Ultimate Empire that you forget some of its vital components. Maybe you forget to make time for the family. Maybe you forget to listen to your employees. Maybe you forget to share info with your partners. Maybe you forget to eat. Maybe you forget about your health. You forget about some of your promises. You forget to get organized. You forget why you're working so hard. You forget to ask for help. You forget to include your team. Or maybe you forgot your anniversary. You forgot he has feelings too. You forgot to be appreciative. You forgot about your own wellbeing. You forgot your priorities. Maybe you forgot who you are. Or maybe, just maybe your forgot what you are capable of.

Time. It seems we don't have enough of it, but I think time is a lot like money. It's not that we don't have enough of it, we just don't want to spend it on something we might regret. I can't promise you that mediation will bring you peace, but it will bring you knowledge. Usually about yourself. And if you do it along enough, and that long enough is completely based on you, it will bring you understanding.

How much time is enough time? 5 minutes, 30

minutes, an hour? I don't know exactly. Whatever you feel comfortable with. Whatever you have time for. But I will say that I think that one should meditate as long as it takes to learn or even remember something. You always want to come away enlightened in some way so that your life experience is enhanced, even by the smallest amount. You may fight this so called necessity. It's cool, I understand. It might seem like a big waste of time to you. You've got things under control. You know exactly what you're doing and what's going on. But do you know how you feel? Do you know what you worry about? Do you know what annoys you? Do you know why she makes you angry? Do you know the origin of your mood swings? Do you know why they complain about you?

People will fight this or even ignore it and we know why. They are too busy. Those same people too busy to meditate are too busy to read and too busy to make their own health a priority. To build the Ultimate Empire you must constantly seek for more understanding of yourself.

Chapter 52
Be Blessed

I want you to know that you are blessed. That you are gifted. That you have been given an advantage. I want you to know that you have access to something special. That you are lucky. How do I know this? Because you know this. Do things always go your way? On the surface, of course not. Neither for me, but they always do on a deeper level. That level comes from GRINDING relentlessly through the bad luck long enough until it turns into your good luck. Until it turns into your lesson. Until it turns into your triumph. Until it turns into your story. There's no such thing as a bad day, only bad moments.

Allow yourself to be blessed. I'm not talking religion, I'm speaking acceptance. Accept that the world is on your side. That it wants you to win and win big. Accept that it's here to back you up every day that you choose to give it your best shot. Accept that you have been given the blueprint for success. You have been blessed with the key to victory. It's unfair how lucky you are. In fact, it's so unfair that you are obligated to get as much out of life as you can so that you may bless the next person. This is your purpose. To bless the next man or woman. To bless the next team. To bless the next family. Be a blessing, not a waste.

Some people feel that they don't deserve success.

And you know what? They are right, they don't. The other person struggling does. So help them. Be their blessing. Be their light. If you dim yourself to blend into the darkness you will never show them the way to salvation. All blessed individuals have been endowed with the responsibility to impact the world around them. You have been commanded to reach your fullest potential because there is a need for it. It is not up to you to decide whether or not you should be more, it is your duty.

We can sometimes get caught up in the sadness of other people. We think about the young girl that was raped by her father. Is she blessed? We think about the families that are stricken by poverty. Are they blessed? We think about the little boy that was born with AIDS. Is he blessed? Those questions are hard to answer. It can be difficult at times to see the blessing in certain situations. That is why I do not focus my thoughts on how blessed someone else may or may not be. I only focus on what my blessings are, otherwise I could become a letdown. This is not about pleasing others, it's about affecting others in a positive way. It's the only way. People misunderstand the act of being overly positive in the darkest of situations. It does not fix the problem, it buffers it. Like wearing a seat belt. It does not prevent the crash, but it sure will minimize the damage it does to you. Be blessed with the Ultimate Empire.

Chapter 53
Alone I stand

Deep in the darkness of an infinite room there, is only one illuminated by the focus of one beam of light. Here is where the champion exists. Alone, isolated, and without distraction. Focused on only the next step, for the champion does not look ahead nor behind. The champion lays her eyes only on the food she is preparing at hand, for she is the stay-at-home mother and her arena is at the home. The champion only recognizes the glow coming from his computer because he is a new business owner and the battle for a piece of the market is led by his diligence. The champion is typically alone. Why? Isn't it obvious? Only the champ is crazy enough to ever want to be one. Only someone obsessed would ever want to be the best. The best is a solo act. It requires one to adapt to the darkness because the world must be shut out. Time is dedicated to improvement. The thought of boredom is pure heaven to a champion for it is simplicity and the Mastery of fundamental skills that make up a champion. Repetition. Repeat. Ingrain the simplistic. Hardwire what you already know. These words were written in the darkness of my mind. The deepest solitude of my soul. Alone, I stand here.

I've seen people become terrified because they have been abandoned by once loyal partners. I've seen men crumble under the pressure of independent thinking. I've seen women disappear, like magic, after the hint of

174

possibility that they are in this thing on their own. Human beings are mainly a herding type of species. They follow the pack. They enjoy the safety of blending in with the crowd and speaking amongst themselves the possibilities that lie outside of the herd, not daring to ever take a chance at leaving though. Why? Because of the existence of the other type of human being. The Wolf. For every thousand people, there is a wolf disguised as a sheep. There is a person looking who looks just like you and me, but is on a different mission than the pack. The Wolf is looking to take advantage of you. It's goal is to confuse you. Convince you that he's one of you sheep and then rob you of your wool when you least suspect it. Sometimes the wolf is so good that you give him your wool willingly thinking it's the right thing. That is how sneaky the wolf can be. And if you're really not careful, the wolf could end up eating all that you are for breakfast.

How do we defend against the Big Bad Wolf? Well, sheep typically run, but not everybody gets away. Fortunately our communities are led by sheep dogs. They come in all sizes, shapes and colors. Some are powerful and some are a little more passive. Some are alert and some may not be as aware. But they are the leaders of the sheep. They represent the direction in which the sheep may go. They stand out from the group but they are not separate from the group. The sheep they lead give them purpose. The herd gives them a place in the universe to operate. Without them they are lost. They are brave at barking orders, yet awfully terrified to ever leave the heard. The sheep dog can pick out a wolf and with the backup of his loyal sheep, can chase the wolf away to which it came. It may be a sheep dog, but they still have sheep attached to the front of their name.

What do sheep, wolves, and sheep dogs have anything to do with building the Ultimate Empire? Nothing of course. Only a human can do that. This is why it is crucial that you understand the place of the shepherd. The shepherd is the mastermind behind it all. He or she is the puppeteer. The sheep dog is merely a subordinate and often times right hand companion to the shepherd. The sheep dog relays information to the sheep that was passed by the shepherd. The sheep dog may alert the shepherd of wolves in the area, but it is typically the shepherd that will ward off enemies. The shepherd uses the sheep for their wool and milk. This is how the shepherd makes a living. He is in command of the machine which provides for himself, his family, as well as the sheep dog and especially for the sheep themselves for without them he cannot build a business. The bigger the shepherds herd is the more money he will bring in, but also the more responsibility and problems he will be burdened with.

The shepherd seems like an awesome position to be in. You get to build an Empire after all, but still only one in a million become shepherds. Why? Because the shepherd is alone. She cannot fully connect with the sheep like a human can with another human. The shepherd bears the wellbeing of every sheep and sheep dog she takes in. She is constantly thinking about how to provide for them all and profit for herself. Keep everyone happy, healthy, and protected. The sheep typically don't deal with the wolves, foxes, and other outsides enemies because the shepherd is usually fighting them off. If not careful, the shepherd can be caught off guard by an enemy and be severely hurt by a wolf. The sheep and the sheep dog do not fully understand the shepherd, they just expect to be fed at the same time every day like clockwork and any variation from this

176

schedule is blamed on the shepherd. The successful shepherd gladly accepts this burden every day because she knows the sheep don't know any better. Nor do they care to ever know. The sheep dog pretends to know. And if they are not taken proper care of or monitored effectively, sometimes even the sheep dog can be found biting at the heels of your sheep.

If you're building the Ultimate Empire and you're serious about this thing, you must be willing to accept the fact that you will be alone. Even when surrounded by hundreds of sheep, you are still alone. And your herd will not always understand what you are and where you are coming from. They only expect to be taken care of for providing you with value with minimal effort. They feel it is their right to be fed by your efforts and resources, and it is. But do not give up hope, because you are not the only shepherd in the land. There are many more out there facing the same challenges and feeling the same pressures. You can connect with these individuals for they share your journey and pain. You can build the Ultimate Empire together.

Chapter 54
Little Voice

No one wants to admit it, but we all have many voices fighting for attention inside of our head. Some we ignore, most we don't even notice. If you feel like you have multiple personalities happening in your brain at one time don't worry, you're normal. I promise you, every single person on the planet is dealing with the same issue, no matter what their life may look like to you on the outside. But the truth is, though your brain may be harboring many people, only one true person exists. This person is called choice.

Becoming wealthy and a dominant force in your career field does not mean that you have found the real you. This is just a version of you. The successful billionaire Real-Estate tycoon is not necessarily any more a person's true self as the drug addict who lives in an abandoned building. They are both destinations that were reached by people who made certain decisions based on the little voices expressing their opinions in their head. In fact, we know this to be true because there are stories of characters going from the bottom to the top and back down to the bottom. Drug addicts who have come to a cross-roads in their lives and turned everything around, creating a life of health, wealth, and prosperity. Rich moguls who built humongous Empires just to see it all crumble due to drugs, infidelity, and unethical business practices. There is nothing different about you and I. There is nothing different about wealth and poverty. The only thing that is different is the decisions that got you where you are. Which little voice did you listen to. We want to say that you should always listen to the voice of reason and sound ethics. But for some reason right and wrong isn't always black and white. For some reason, wrong can sometimes feel right. That's tough to manage.

What's right and wrong? I'm not completely sure. I have an idea, but my perception is irrelevant because you will do what you feel you must do anyway. The real question is what do you believe is right and wrong? And maybe you're not sure either. That is why married couples fall victim to temptation. Adultery they call it. Affairs they call it. There are different reasons why we do it. But why do we *choose* to do it? Because of that little voice. That little voice telling us we need more adventure and excitement. That little voice telling you your spouse doesn't appreciate you anymore. That little voice saying you're in love. It's that same little voice that tells potential Shepherds to be just sheep because they are not worthy of controlling an Empire. It was another little voice that told International Bestselling author Paulo Coelho to write books for the world to read. We follow whichever voice is loudest and most persistent in our heads.

So, the key is to understand who you want to be, not who you are. You are who you are based on your environment, parents, experiences, and habits. Who you become is based on what you decide from here on out. If you want to become CEO of a Fortune 500 company, begin to read books written by fortune 500 CEO's. If you want to become an Olympic Swimmer, study successful Olympic Swimmers. If you want to be an All-Star father to your kids, copy what you think are All-Star qualities from other

179

dads. Don't try to build a life based on what you think is necessary in your own imagination. Our brains innately want to do good things. Study what is good. Read what is good. Listen to audios consisting of good information. Go to good seminars. Observe life with the intention of finding more good in it. Yes evil, what we generally consider as evil, will appear. Thoughts of doing evil will arrive. Temptation will follow. I will not tell you to not to participate, you will make that choice all on your own. But I want you to know that your decision will be influenced by what is most clear to your mind. What makes the most sense to you? If you can't see clearly why you should start your own business, you won't. If you can't see clearly why you need to go to an AA meeting for your alcoholism, you won't. Time is always ticking against you, if you want to make the desired decision or even change your life around, start absorbing the desired information now.

Here's a question. What information are you feeding your team, your family, your partners, your colleagues, or even your fans? This goes for verbally, visually, morally, ethically, spiritually, and productively. How are you helping them to understand you? Can they clearly see your vision? Do they have the tools and resources necessary to stay the course and not be deterred or are they out in the ocean on their own? Are you helping them or expecting them to figure it out? Do they know not what they do? Don't assume just because they are adults that they know what to do. A lot of times in fact, we assume children know what to do. Is it sad, I don't know. But it seems impractical. I feel it to be illogical. Do you understand me? To build the Ultimate Empire, the people in it must have the right, clear cut information in their heads, because if left to their own thinking those little voices might send them somewhere they never intended to be.

Chapter 55
Rely On No One

This is a tough one. It almost seems contradictory. I feel like up until this point I have harped on the importance of other people being in sync with you and your vision in order to build the Ultimate Empire. The idea is to understand your own negative and self-opposing thoughts. Understand that these are the same thoughts going through everybody else head, and understand how you should think and help others think the same way as well. The purpose is to get the people in your life, on your team, in your family, part of your company, all on the same accord. That is the point. Then why in the world would I tell you to rely on no one and only count on yourself. Because in the end, beginning and middle of the day you are the only one aware of what you're thinking and the same goes for everybody else.

Now hypothetically, yes you have to trust people. Meaning, you do have to give people a shot. Why? Because you can't do it alone. There are just certain things you can't do or can't do well enough. There are certain activities that are important but you just don't have the time to execute them. Nobody is omnipresent no matter how much it may seem that they are. No one can do it all, but you can do the most.

One night as an Uber driver, I picked up a young

lad from his job. He was a manager at one of the eateries in Busch Gardens, an amusement park. He told how he had been working there for a little over 7 year since he got out of High School. With no college degree, he was able to work his way up the ladder and even had college graduates working under him. How is this possible? It is simple, he had more experience and knowledge on how to run the restaurant efficiently. He had worked in every position within the joint. He knew how to be the cook, the decorator, the cashier, and the server. He knew how to clean and break it all down. He knew how to close and how to open. He knew what was expected of him and what the customers desired. He knew how to provide an awesome experience for his guest. He knew this and his superiors knew it as well. That is why they not only put him in that position but also paid for him to go back to school and receive his business degree. They believed in him because they knew something very vital. They knew that he didn't need to rely on anyone to get the job done.

We need people in our sphere of influence who will push us up to the next level. Desperately we need that. We need awesome people on our team to take our vision and performance to the next level. But I know this fact more than anything else: People will let you down, in multiple ways.

They may lie to you. They may come up short. They may change their minds. They may make a mistake. They may not know what to do. They may not show up. They may get distracted. They may not believe in you. They may get tired. They may quit. They may be wrong. They may do any of these things, and they will. Almost everybody will do at least one of these things to let you down. And typically it's by accident believe it or not. This is not to be pessimistic, these are just facts. Does that mean we should do everything ourselves? My way or the highway? No, we should just be aware that we need to be ready at all times to pick up the slack.

Use people. Not abuse, but utilize their gifts, talents, skills, knowledge, wisdom and generosity. Use it because everybody wants to feel useful. But do not rely on them. Do not make them the make or break factor. Understand that unforeseen issues may arise. May or may not be their fault but they may still be a part of the problem. Must you get rid of them? I don't know. I just know you will have to adapt. You will need to respond and do it quickly, typically. Especially in a business setting.

You are the most reliable person alive when it comes to building your Ultimate Empire. Even if you're not the most talented, you are still most important because no one will put in the effort necessary to make happen like you. No one else will fight hard enough on your behalf in order to make your dreams happen. It's you, it always been you, and it will forever be you. Let your spouse know that too. Inform your children, so that they are not so easily disappointed by future let downs. Let your team know that they are Masters of their own ship. A ship I call Destiny. No one has ever had an Empire built in their honor. Maybe passed down to them, but never for the purpose of them. And it will not happen today. Keep GRINDING.

Chapter 56
The Ultimate Fighter

The ultimate fighter is you. That would be a very predictable and unexciting way to explain it. "We are all the Ultimate fighter. The ultimate fighter lives within us all." I'm sorry, but that's just not true. The ultimate fighter lives in the real world where challenges, misfortune, and traumatic experiences take place. The ultimate fighter is active in the hustle and bustle of the world no matter what recent success or failure has been witnessed. The ultimate warrior is the greatest winner of them all. All they do is win or are in the midst of battling for their next victory.

Take, for example, Kevin Hart, aka "The Comedic Rock star." He is arguably the funniest man in the world right now, and for good reason. A) He's a hilarious standup comic B) He's always on the road and C) He is everywhere doing everything. Kevin Hart, the genius funny man, has essentially made himself omnipresent. He's on television, on social media, in movies, doing standup, hosting award shows, making YouTube videos and just doesn't seem to stop. Kevin is the definition of a warrior. He is always suited up and ready to tackle the next challenge. He hasn't gotten comfortable yet. Why? Because he's reached fame, but hasn't built the Ultimate Empire.

I'm writing a 90 chapter book. Notice I say writing and not written for at this point I haven't finished writing

184

this thing. I choose my words wisely and my philosophies with care. My phrases all mean something. Anyone can write about 90 different ideas all saying the same thing, all meaning the same thing, all pointing to the same conclusion. This is not one of those types of books because life is not that kind of player. Each challenge for you is unique and specific. I don't care if this is your hundredth time being in this situation or if everybody you know has gone through it. The next problem is a different problem all together. So understand this, it is extremely important that you know who the real ultimate fighter is, because in reality we are all fighters at some point in our lives. When we get into a bind and situations get tough we are sometimes forced to step up to the plate to fight for our very survival. You see? There is nothing special about a fighter. We are all fighters. The ultimate fighter however is not just a fighter. She or he is a warrior.

There's a reason why the rich get richer and the poor get poorer. The rich are warriors. They go looking for the fight. They go searching for new territory to conquer. They are always in fight mode even when they are obviously winning by a land slide. Fighting for a mission is a constant state for the warrior. And if a warrior has nothing to fight for, they die. Figuratively and sometimes literally. A good example is the late Joe Paterno, once crowned College Football's most winningest coach in the history of the NCAA. Coached at Penn State for 61 years before he was fired. He passed away 2 months later at age 85. Technically he had lung cancer, but I also think that it's safe to say that his will to live on died the same day he was stripped of his right to coach college football. He had nothing left to fight for.

The warrior is proactive, the fighter is reactive.

Fighters respond to dire situations. They are often content with the way things are and just hope that nothing goes wrong in the near future forcing them to fight once again. Fighters do just enough to not lose it all. Fighters think warriors only exist because they are talented or lucky and think everything goes their way. Warriors believe all of their riches can be stripped away from them at any time because they know life is ruthless and unbiased in it's unfair nature. Though it is true that not all fighters are warriors, they all have the potential to be. Sometimes with the right push from a coach, the slight nudge from a spouse, the super charge from a book, or even the magic spark lit by a speaker, a content individual can turn into a motivated SOB seeking blood in the name of self-victory. This is the type of person that wants to get better. These are the type of people that improve well beyond expected by their peers. Not the talented, but instead the relentless. Empires are guarded by warriors.

Chapter 57
Help Is Coming

Though it is true that in order to build the Ultimate Empire you need an incredible team, there is first a catch to the creation of that team. You must first reflect the traits of an incredible leader. You must first represent the qualities of a hard worker. You must first take on the characteristics of an Empire builder otherwise you will lose peoples interest and they will move on to help somebody else build their dreams. So this one goes out to all my 24/7 GRINDERS out there putting in the time to grow, learn, and take risks. Help is on its way.

Did you know that people want to help you build your Empire? It's true. Out of the 7 billion selfish individuals all trying to fend for themselves and put food on the table, almost all of them want to take time out of their day to help your achieve greatness. How is this possible when you know for a fact that no one is willing to step out on a limb for you, not even your own family? Because I know that everyone wants a job, everyone want to get paid, everyone wants to win, everyone want to watch winners and everybody is a consumer.

Consciously, no. No one wants to help you build a beautiful life because they want their life to be beautiful. But subconsciously they do want your business to be successful because they want a job that is reliable and

187

looking to hire. Your wife wants a man who is financially stable, as well as emotionally. Your parents want a daughter that is healthy and happy. Your players want to play on a winning team. No matter who you are or where you are trying to go, somebody will always benefit from your success and they want desperately for you to win in that category. If you win, they win.

Here is the other component to your future success. Have you ever noticed that when somebody is giving their absolute best effort into something, really trying with all of their might to achieve a very specific result, that there is something inside of us that compels one to give them a helping hand. Have you ever done that? Saw someone really struggling to make things happen, and because of your knowledge or resources you know you can be of some sort of service. So you take the time to advise, to share, and to support for no other reason than to help. Just because you want to see them win. You don't want to see their hard work go to waste. You don't want to see effort be given in vain. Think deeply about that moment. That moment when you felt empathy and showed compassion. Now, think of the moments when somebody was just looking for a hand out because they were to lazy to do it on their own. Think of all those people out there who are trying to get over on you, cheat you, or take advantage of the system. Most of us don't feel so compelled to help those type of people. We know nothing positive or productive will come of it. The victim will forever be the victim no matter how much aid you provide. Only the warrior can put outside support to good use. So ask yourself this question. Which person are you?

If you're the hard nose, ground and pound victor that I know you are then I have awesome news for you.

188

Help is coming.

It's on the way right now as we speak, or you read. The person you've been looking for, the answer to all of you're problems is on the way, you just have to hold on long enough for them to reach you. If you quit now they will never reach you. They are looking for you. Searching for somebody to be a blessing too. They will only know who it is when they meet you in the middle of your grind. They will not recognize the slackers. They will not notice the excuses. They will be oblivious to the ones that gave up. Your supporters can only see those in action and if you give up now they will walk right pass you. You have to stay on their radar. You have to work, study, research, build, stretch and grow with all of your might because someone wants to come to your aid; they just need proof first that you are the real deal. They just want to make sure that their assistance will not be in vein. Phil Knight, the Founder of Nike, did not successfully build the biggest sportswear company in the world because he had a better shoe than Adidas and Puma. He was successful because he never stopped believing he could be the best. He never stopped grinding it out even when it seemed his company was about to go under. That inspired the people around him to give up their time and their own paychecks just to keep the dream alive. Help is coming. Not only do you need to know that, but also make sure your team knows. Your family needs to know that. We all want to feel that somebody is on our side. Let them know that you are on their side. Lead by example and I guarantee the cavalry will come running when the time is right. The Ultimate Empire will be yours.

Chapter 58
It Gets Easier

As a personal trainer, I tell my clients all the time "You will feel pretty sore after the first session. You might even feel dizzy and light headed, but if you keep at it the road to fitness gets easier." Does that make sense? Maybe you'll understand it from an education perspective. When you are entering High School, the first year is usually the most confusing. You have to adapt to a new environment filled with students who are up to 3-4 years older than you, but still considered your peers. You are entering a monster that will chew you up and spit you out if you're not careful. Girls grow boobs and boys have some hair under their arm pits now. Writing standards are higher. Subjects are taught by different teachers. You must travel from class to class in an environment where seniors reign supreme. They look like trees to you, and unless you have Google maps you may get lost in the forest of kids while trying to reach your next destination before the bell rings. Your hormones are raging, your interests are shifting, and your views about the world are maturing. You are being given a whole new level of responsibility and you are expected to adjust with ease. Jokes are made and teenagers can be cruel. Cliques are created. College is that much closer and adulthood is right around the corner. Freshman year can make you or break you. And if you can survive the first year, sophomore year gets a whole lot smoother.

Practice makes perfect. Some will argue perfect practice will make perfect. I think that's just somebody being picky. Practice definitely makes you better, right? Yes, especially when you practice hard with a deliberate intent to become better. And what happens when you practice with that specific need to improve in mind? The game gets easier.

What I'm explaining here is nothing new. I have not uncovered some deep, dark hidden secret that was lost during medieval times. What I am telling you is a fact that not only holds true at your job, in business, in school and in sports. But it also holds true in marriage, parenthood, wealth building, leadership, sales, and entrepreneurship.

Most phenomenal workers understand that the job gets easier with time. Where the challenge lies is in making the average workers realize that as well, and convincing them to do their best now for the great results tomorrow. This is where people trip up. Governing people.

As a brand new entrepreneur with a start up the road is hard. And as you progress and grow it gets even harder. It has a different curve than other everyday adventures. It does not get easier the next day, it's only just getting started. If you're trying to build something big and self-sustaining, it will get harder year after year before you ever reach a point where the business gets easier. That's why most people quit. They can't see the light at the end of the tunnel. Same goes for marriage. Most do not build a greater understanding and connection with their spouse as time goes on. They actually, typically, grow further apart. Becoming more and more distant, not really knowing why they can't connect. But for those who are willing to stick in there long enough, learn to compromise, and grow with their life partner, the road does become easier in due time.

The same goes for sales, building wealth and especially developing leadership. When you're new to sales and you don't have a knack for it, that's tough. And every NO you get makes it tougher. The weak parish, but the strong survive and eventually thrive. When building wealth, your first six figures is tough. And your first million seems almost impossible. But once you get there you realize how simple it really is, at least that's what they tell me. And here is where your Ultimate Empire is predicated on. LEADERSHIP. The ability to point people in the right direction, put them in the most effective position, persuade them on how it will work out, convince them that you're worth following, clearly show them how it's done, and uphold a certain level of respect. That my friends, is hard to do and takes an extremely long time to master. But it get easier, at some point.

Chapter 59
Be A Hero

I have found that most men are waiting to be saved, like some damsel in distress. Lol. And most women think that they will be saved when they get married. At some point, both realize that they will not be saved. Even if someone were to scoop you up and virtually wash all of your problems, issue, and challenges away, you still would be in danger. In danger from what is missing inside of your own mind.

Remember the financial crash of 2009? Yeah you do. Remember how the government bailed out all of those banks? Trillions of dollars spent to save the economic abusers of America. The red-handed Real Estate Bubble blowers who got away with it. Yeah, you know who I'm talking about. Fortunately for them, they were blessed to be given the financial backing to prop themselves up on to continue existing within the American culture. It saved alot of jobs. But it didn't save everybody's job, and it definitely didn't save everyone's home.

Big company layoffs. Foreclosures. Government shutdowns. Stock market crashes. Industry bubbles. Application rejections. Denying University letters. Non-paying internships. Robberies. Cancer. Diabetes. Heart attacks. Suspensions. Expulsion. DUI. Overdose. Natural disasters. Racism. Sexism. Adultery. Juvenile delinquency.

Convicted felon. Teen pregnancy. Bankruptcy. Failing program. Sibling passed away. Public embarrassment. Misled. Fired. Homeless. ADD. ADHD. Depression. Alcoholic. Drug addict. Who's going to save you when you fall victim?

There are people every day committing suicide, not because they are poor. Not because they've had a hard life. Not because the system is unfair. But because they're life is too perfect. WTF. First world problems.

There can only be one true hero in anybody's life. Sure your parents can be your hero. Your mentor can guide you down the path known as the light side. A fireman can rescue you from a burning building. Yes, people outside of you can be incredibly beneficial to your life. But I will tell you one thing. None of them, no matter how much they love you, will be able to create success for you. None of them can inject fulfillment into your fibers. No one can manifest your deepest desires. Nobody can bring to you happiness. Not a single person can do it. Only you can do it.

The hero you've been reading about in the stories, watching on the big screen, hearing about on the streets. The man or woman that you've dreamed of, wished for, that special someone, your savior. That person has always been you. Only you can avoid negative people that could ultimately stifle your growth. Only you can become a student of love, communication, and success. Only you can put in the time and effort to build a Brand, a company, a following, or a family. Only you can dictate what you allow into your body and how well it is taken care of. Only you can learn about money. Only you can understand what it means to be a leader. Only you can direct your thoughts in the most productive direction. Only you can Master your craft .Only you can figure out what YOU want. It's a YOU thing. People can temporarily step in to assist, but they can't shield you from yourself. Your own shortcomings and downfalls. Your own demons and sins. They cannot save you from your own guilt or depression or even greed. It's on you and what you decide to do every moment that you breathe. Your Empire is led by one person. You.

Chapter 60
Your Ego, Your Failure

E.G.O. Energy Going Out. What kind of EGO are you emitting into the Earth's atmosphere? What kind of energy are you sharing with the world? Are you sharing any of it at all with the world? Maybe you're an introvert. I bet you think you're not putting out any energy towards the universe, let alone any specific individual. On the contrary, you are forever letting out vibes. You are a direct force on people's lives. To think not and belittle yourself is to let your "Ego" get in the way of your success. Oh, I bet you didn't see that one coming.

When you speak of ego, people usually think of someone that is cocky or full of themselves. Egotistical they call it. Unless you win. When you're a winner, you're just confident. That's just your swag. When you're a champion, it's considered a winner sedge. Having a winning mentality. Until you lose and then you fall back down from grace to once again be known as the egotistical bastard that got too cocky and lost it all just like we predicted. What a confusing world.

To tell you the truth I don't know what the "Ego" really is. I'm not even sure if it's a real thing. But if I were to place it anatomically on a person, I would say that the "Ego mind" is the conscious mind. In turn I would call our subconscious mind our GOD mind. And then finally our

196

body is the instinctive/primate mind. Are all necessary? Who knows, but they are all present and very real, that I assure you. It is also important to know that we only truly control one sector of this love triangle. The dreaded EGO.

Energy going out. Ego is thought and thoughts are pure energy. This energy commands the body and directs the subconscious. At the same time the primordial mind, which runs off of chemical reactions happening within the body, is constantly sending signals to the subconscious creating certain thought patterns which are then analyzed by the Ego. And this is how the Ego makes most of it's decisions. Based on the signal sent to the subconscious mind. So since we cannot control the animal mind for it operates off of natural instinct, we can only hope to send another set of signals to our subconscious mind. This will hopefully be used to combat certain unwanted thoughts of immediate gratification and be replaced with thoughts of long term achievement.

To give into the subconscious is not to give into failure. To give into the instinctive, reactive, and primate mind without properly weighing out the options can result in failure. The smaller the decision window, the higher the pressure. The more significant and critical the choice is, the more critical it is for your Ego mind to have the long term beneficial signals being sent to it.

If you think your current Ego mind is capable of making all correct decisions without the help of mentorship, companionship, reading, research, experience and experimentation, then your ego mind will surely fail you in the building of the Ultimate Empire. And if by some chance you get it. You understand the importance of lifelong learning and improvement, you will also learn that the same difficulty of self-Ego awareness stretches far across the world, including your family, boyfriend, girlfriend, manager, students, teammates, babysitter, and clients. Their egos are influenced by yours and if you want to be a successful leader then make sure your conscious mind is emitting thoughts that coincide with the vibrations of your Ultimate Empire.

Chapter 61
One Dream

I hope I have you dreaming again. I hope I have you imagining awesome adventures again. Just like when you were a child. I hope you have that twinkle in your eye. That spark in your brain. That fire in your belly. That hunger in your soul. I hope it's overwhelming you right now, because that's what the Ultimate Empire is derived from. That is your blue print, your dreams. And not just the ideas you have resting on your heart, but that one big vision that you cannot shake. That's what you need to know. That's all you need to see. Here, is where your focus must lie, because if you're like most people who say "I have a lot of dreams" you will never realize any of them.

Let's be really meticulous about this one. Can you have multiple dreams? Yes. Can you accomplish multiple dreams? Yes. Can you work on them at the same time? Yes. Can you have massive success during the pursuit of your multiple dream expedition? No. Why? Because dreams are the seemingly impossible. Meaning, there is no conceivable way to achieve them in a normal, ordinary, average person way. You have to do paranormal type of things which require an inhuman like focus.

Can you have multiple goals? Yes, and you should. Goals can be big or small. You should have a list of both. And they should always be attainable on some measurable scale. Why? Because these goals are your stepping stones to your dream. Perfect example, ME. Your author. Mel Jones, your Powerful Thinking Coach. The Motivational Philosopher. The BEAST. Whatever you want to call me. My dream used to be for me to one day become an NFL player. I got as far as becoming a full scholarship Running Back for a DIAA college football program. I had this dream from age 7 all the way up to age 23. And though I thought about my dream every day, I did not focus on it. I focused on the task at hand. The day in front of me. The next game. The current practice. The very rep I was pushing in the weight room. So if you even want to come remotely close to achieving such a seemingly impossible achievement, according to the average person, you have to A) remind yourself of that dream and B) create a pyramid of goals that trickle down into your present moment.

So for me the star at the top of my tree was the NFL. Before that comes college. Before that comes doing well enough in high school to receive a scholarship. Before that was making the High School Varsity Team. Before that was playing middle school ball. Before that was pop warner. Before that was putting on pads for the first time, learning the game, going over the fundamentals, and practicing every day. And each day, as I grew older I had a new goal set for that day. A new focus for that practice. I wanted to be the best in practice today. I wanted to hit the hardest. I wanted run the fastest. I wanted to score the most touchdowns. When it came to game day, it was all just routine. I wanted the best stats. But even those little pop warner games were in result of how successfully I practiced the 6 days before hand.

They say the Jack of all Trades is a Master of none. That is somewhat true. You can't become a Master in multiple industries at the same time, but it is still highly imperative that you are highly efficient in many areas within your industry if you hope to ever become a Master of the Ultimate Empire. Amazon might be a Master at providing people with the best priced items found online, but they also are great at fast delivery, customer satisfaction, guaranteed order fulfillment, restocking items, proficient packaging, and getting quality products from credible sources. A Master painter is nothing if he doesn't know where to get a supply of all the colors.

Why are people lazy? Usually because they either don't have a dream to inspire them or they have too many dreams which paralyze them from taking any meaningful and consistent action. And let me provide you with a little secret. Your dream doesn't have to be yours. That goes for your team, your partners, and your family. We don't all need our own individual dream in order to be motivated to GRIND. We can borrow someone else's dream. If you sell your dream effectively to your people, they will go to hell and back for you. Why? Because they now see where they fit in your dream. They see how it is possible. They understand the pay off. They know its the right thing to do. One dream, one Ultimate Empire.

Chapter 62
Uncomfortable vs. Exhaustion

Get comfortable with being uncomfortable. A common phrase that has become very popular in today's self-development culture. An oxymoron, but it makes sense. It is the idea that you operate on a day-to-day basis looking to do the tasks you don't feel like doing. Searching for activities that you are unfamiliar with yet you know are crucial for you to complete. It is the understanding that you must participate in new situations, difficult scenarios, and deal in stressful circumstances. Why? Because the Ultimate Empire is literally a living, breathing organism and is constantly being attacked by outside forces that threaten its very survival and growth. If you're not growing then you are surely dying, and that growth only takes place when you struggle through something. You can't build muscle without pushing your body through resistance and you can't gain intellect without stressing your mind with new information. Your Empire requires constant push in order to break through the concrete flower bed.

Being uncomfortable is a given. Being tired is inevitable. Being exhausted is a whole different topic.

The word exhausted is defined as being drained of

one's physical and mental resources. To be completely used. In a literal sense, when have you ever been pushed to the point that you have been completely used up?

And here is where the rubber meets the road. Society, at least in America, has reached a point to where we feel entitled to success. We feel we deserve long vacations, short work weeks, high pay, little responsibility, and a high leadership status. We believe our spouse should do more for us, our children are our property, and our friends should be looking out for us around the clock. We "think" that we work "extremely hard." We pretend that we are constantly going above and beyond for other people with no fair amount of reciprocity. We act like the world owes us a favor. How is that? Because the average person is tired and being tired puts you in a state of uncomfortability.

Most people want to live in the Ultimate Empire but they rather not do the things that make them feel uncomfortable in order to get it. Unfortunately, this awesome plan of ours does not save one from being uncomfortable. In fact, you are probably even more uncomfortable not living your dreams. You feel uncomfortable with your job, with your marriage, with your degree, with your colleagues, with your pets, with your bills, with your paychecks, or just the direction your life is going. It makes you cringe just thinking about all the things your life is missing. So why don't you do something about it? What's the real reason you won't read that book or run those 2 miles? Fear is definitely one reason, another is fatigue. And as some would say after a long day's work, "I'm exhausted."

Are you really exhausted or are you just tired? Have

you completely spent all of your energy as well as all of your body's reserves? Is there truly nothing left in the tank? Let me put it this way, are you dying?

If the answer is no, then get to work! If it's yes, you better hurry up and accomplish something meaningful because your time is running out. I'm serious about that last part.

The word exhausted has been tossed around so frivolously that people think of it as being synonymous with the word tired. Like, being a little energy drained and being completely spent of all reserves is somehow the same thing. It's a copout. It's a logical reasoning in people's heads for why they can't complete the necessary actions in order to take their lives from getting by to the start of a dynasty. I know college kids on summer break who can sleep all day, show up to the gym midafternoon, and before they can even change into their gym clothes can describe to me the overwhelming feeling of exhaustion that has overcome their body. From doing NOTHING.

The successful entrepreneurs. The ones whose business doesn't flop in the first 5 years. They work 24/7, 365. The President of the United States. He has no clock out time. There are no lunch breaks. He doesn't just manage over a store or 2. A family here and there. He is responsible for an entire country and is leading the whole free world.

You want to talk about an exhausting job. You think being a parent of a few kids is tough. Trying raising 10. How about 12. I know a family like that, what a mad house. Oh, you're a High School teacher. You deal with hormonal teenagers all day and grade papers all night. Say that to the High School Head Football Coach. He spends an extra 2-5 hours after school directing a group of young men to greatness and is still responsible for being a competent educator.

Do you feel me? It's perspective. A perspective that most people never see. It's not until you recognize somebody else's struggles or become forced to deal with a new pressure that pushes you beyond any past limits, that you find out that you are not truly exhausted. You're just uncomfortable. You just don't feel like doing another rep. You're just conditioned to believe that, because you have a full time job and some responsibilities, you are allowed to claim exhaustion and lie dormant in your growth. We all know people like that. I hope you're not one of them.

Don't be to hard on them or even yourself. It's not your fault. It's our nature. Human nature. It's our culture. It's the perfect excuse, but excuses don't build Empires. Your team must understand this. Your family has to be hip to it. You have to lead by example. Show what it means to push past tired. To live in the land of the uncomfortable. Become a walking testament and not all, but the ones you need, will follow your lead. They will help you build the Ultimate Empire.

Chapter 63
Harder and Smarter

In order to get paid you must work. In order to get paid above the minimum you must work smart. In order to get paid above the average, you must work hard. In order to get paid in a month what most people get paid in a year, you must work harder and smarter than the average person. You must become a double edged sword bent on slicing your way through the jungle we call "THE STRUGGLE."

I first heard this term from one of my secret mentors Gary Vaynerchuk (he doesn't know he's my mentor yet.). Gary Vee, Serial Entrepreneur and Owner of VaynerMedia, is a super successful entrepreneur and social media icon who has dedicated his life to the HUSTLE. Not because he wants to be rich, but because he loves the game. He enjoys the struggle. He loves turmoil. He is a born warrior who gets a high on the 24/7 grind-a-thon. Basically, he works extremely harder than the average individual. But there are those who claim and have commented to Gary that they don't feel that they need to work that hard. Why? Because they are working smarter. Gary's response, "I work harder and smarter, NOW WHAT DICK!?" Awesome response.

Simply, what he means is that he's not just spinning his wheels endlessly. He puts in ridiculous amount of hours on productive activities that are constantly helping others, constantly providing value, and constantly growing his company, brand, and bank account. He's doing what the best in the world do. Utilizing his time to the fullest to maximize his return on living.

Now, to keep it frank, I am in no way telling you that you should work 19 hour days like Gary Vee throughout the year. That is just not practical for most people. It's not even healthy for most people. Maybe not even for Gary. What I'm really telling you is that if you want the build something greater than just a surviving business; If you want to have more than just a routine marriage; If you want to enjoy a greater relationship with your children unparalleled to the one they have with their friends, you are going to have to be incredibly smart with your hard work.

To work hard is simple. It's to put in extra hours at the office. It's too go above and beyond to make your girlfriend happy. It's giving every sprint your best effort. It's taking time out of your day, no matter how you feel, to write the next chapter in your book. It's doing volunteer work when you don't have any time to spare. It's reading the books because you know it is better to work on yourself more than on your business. That's what working REALLY hard is. Doing the things that most people won't in order to get won't most people will never have. Now how do you combine that with working smarter?

First off, you don't waste time because you know that time is the only commodity you can't buy back. Therefore you schedule your time and are ready to adjust your activities if the schedule changes. Second, you take care of your priority areas on a daily. These include your health, wealth, fitness, knowledge of current events, reflection, professional practice, and learning something from others. Third, always make sure your current actions are in line with you accomplishing your endgame. And if you don't have an endgame, AKA dream, then get one otherwise you will wind up anywhere. And lastly, always look for ways to improve. I promise you your competitor, your teammate, your rival, and your boss, is always looking for areas to be better in. Even your family is unconsciously searching for someone better and if you're always improving, guess what? You will always bet that person they are looking for.

The most successful bodybuilders in the world understand the amount of dedication and hard work it takes to become a champion. They understand the amount of time you must sacrifice in order to potentially be crowned as one of the best. Most have full-time jobs. But they also are aware of the major importance of nutrition and sleep. They may work extremely hard, but they must also be extremely smart with how they utilize their time around their training. Most people don't understand all the components it requires to be great at any one particular thing. Even being champion of the world requires being incredibly awesome in more than one area within one discipline.

You can work hard and never see your Empire grow past the first floor. You can be smart and build a mock Empire that looks nice on the outside, but is vulnerable in it's foundation. The bulk of your Ultimate Empire will be built by tough hands and will reach heights only as high as your thoughts can think it. Work harder and smarter.

Chapter 64
Self-Education 101

The one thing I pride myself above all is that I am a student of success. I intensely study those who have reached greatness before me. I look to reverse engineer the process, the progress, and the failures. I watch for trends and common denominators. I research their history and how they have gotten to where they are. I study the old and the new. I even learn from the dead. I know that education is the most important factor when it comes to success. You must learn from the folks before you. From those who have done it prior. There is no need to reinvent the wheel, just change the model of the car.

Education is the most important asset you will ever have at your disposal. Unfortunately, most of us believe that education only comes from the school system. On the contrary, schools, colleges and universities are typically the least useful forms of educational systems. Typically because they do not inform students on experience. They focus on theory. They give a general knowledge of facts. Or, they make you an expert in a limited field like Engineering. But none of these institutions teach you how to build the Ultimate Empire. What do I mean? They don't teach you how to love. They don't teach you how to raise a family or mentor a child. They don't teach you how to build a multi-billion dollar company or how to become a Best-Selling Author. They don't teach you how to make friends or how to win your boss over. They don't teach you how to provide value to people. They don't teach you how to create a startup. They don't teach you how to save for retirement or how to become a CEO. They don't teach you how to listen to people's problems and help them get through a crises. They don't teach you how to express yourself or how to deal with your emotions. They don't teach you work ethic. They don't teach you how to find your purpose. They don't teach you about success or how to get rich. They don't teach you about what is the healthiest lifestyle. They don't teach you about responsibility. They don't teach you how to win.

You learn predominantly through experience. But hold on, there's a shortcut. You can also learn through other peoples experiences. Woah! Mind blown.

You can literally pick up a book and read on any and every topic imaginable. How do you think classes are taught? Out of somebodies book! You want to learn about leadership, go pick up a book by the expert John C. Maxwell. You want to learn how to read body language? Try *Signals* by Allan Pease. What about *How to Win Friends and Influence People* by Dale Carnegie? Or *Think and Grow Rich* by Napoleon Hill. Maybe you need to learn how to Sell or even close the deal. Try *The Closer's Survival Guide* by Grant Cardone. Is Network Marketing your nitch? Look up *Go Pro* by Eric Worre. Oh, lets not forget learning how to please your spouse. Read The *5 Love Languages* by Gary Chapman.

And the list goes on, and on, and on, and on. In fact, the list grows every year. Possibly every day. I heard someone once tell me that all the knowledge that's in those books can be found in the Bible. Though I'm not one to say that the Bible is not an adequate piece of literature, I will say that if it were all that was needed than all of our problems and questions would have been answered by now.

You want to be a mathematician, study math. You want to be a Lawyer, study law. You want to be an IT specialist, take computer courses. But if you want to be a National Championship coach, no classroom in the world can prepare your mind for that. You will need to learn about how to be an effective leader, how to run a team, how to recruit talent, how to connect with your players, how to delegate responsibility to your staff, how to create a winning culture and how to motivate as well as inspire your team to dream big. You will need to know how to make people work extremely hard for you. Your experience alone won't get you there. You are going to need a lot of help.

Your people will need that type of guidance and mentoring as well. If you are the leader, if you are the light in the family, if you are the boss, then you need to be not only the commander, but an open book of wisdom as well. What better way to learn than from the source. Sometimes we are the source for other people. Maybe you are the source for your peers. Maybe you need to take you and your team to an Eric Thomas conference or a Brendon Burchard seminar. Maybe you need to shadow someone. Maybe you're a successful speaker who needs to hire a speaking coach to go from good to great. You see the learning process never stops.

They say the master never stops learning. Only a fool would believe that they know enough. Only a misguided person would think that they have an adequate amount of information to run the rest of their life with. Without fresh information flowing into your consciousness, you will stop your growth. And as I said once before, anything not growing is surely dying. Don't let your

Empire die.

Chapter 65
Study the Game

In order to truly be a student of the game you must study the game. If you want to be a teacher, you get your Masters in Education. If you want to be a personal trainer, you get your certification. Do you understand? When you want a certain result it requires a certain action and it usually only takes you completing that action once. Now, here is where we gain a greater understanding of the Ultimate Empire. It inherits greatness. It implies Mastery. It feeds on excellence. It resembles perfection. In other words, you have seen many of figures who have seemed to reach a level of phenomenality that makes us believe that they are somewhat like Gods. But you and I know that they are not Gods, merely mortals who have dominated their space and have attained incredible levels of success in that sector or in their life. So if you and I want to reach such levels of efficiency in our lives, who should we get our education from? The Masters.

Study the game. Meaning, analyze your competitors, mentors, idols, peers, and those who have failed. Watch their movements. Learn their philosophies. Decode their language. Gain a deeper understanding. If you want to be a teacher then go to a University. If you want to be the MOST effective teacher then go to an effective educator. If you want to get a job on Wall Street, get a Business degree. If you want to run a Fortune 500 company, read the books of people of have done it.

Did you know that running a successful relationship is a game? The game of love I suppose. I've been studying it for quite some time now and I've come across some important factors when dealing with happy and unhappy relationships/marriages. Here is what makes a relationship fulfilling:

1) Seduction
2) Intimacy
3) Communication
4) Understanding
5) Vision
6) Attraction
7) Growth
8) Sex
9) Security
10) Attention
11) Affirmation
12) Support
13) Roles
14) Adventure
15) Independence
16) Goals
17) Connection
18) Peace
19) Spontaneity
20) ?

Didn't I tell you that I'm a student of the game? I've studied love and relationships so thoroughly that I now understand that there is still more to learn. This isn't even a love thing, it's a success principle. That is why I put a question mark on the last part, because I know within you lies the key ingredient to having the perfect relationship.

How closely do you study your opponent? How deeply do you dig into the philosophy of your industry? Sam Walton spent all of his entrepreneur life studying other retail and discount stores. Didn't matter if he was overseas or in the United States of America. Didn't matter if it was Target or Kmart. He was always learning and watching out for that key product he was missing. Or maybe a better layout of panty hose on aisle 3. Or the distance between the racks of merchandise. Sam went so far as too fly himself in a not so safe one man airplane, from location to location, making certain that each Walmart was up to par and the customers were well taken care of.

Study the game. Study who's on your team. What are their strengths and weaknesses? What motivates them? What do they want to achieve? What role best suits them? Is their performance matching up to their own personal standards? Do they trust you? How can you build the Ultimate Empire if you don't know your people, your family, your employees, your partners, or your customers?

I don't think I told you this but….Rome wasn't built in a day and all Empires will eventually fall if not properly taken care of. What builds them is what keeps them afloat. Evolution. Adaptation. Innovation. You can't evolve if you stay the same. You cannot adapt if you're not open to change. You will not innovate if you do not understand what is missing. Study the game and all of its inner workings.

Chapter 66
Speak With Conviction

It's easier said than done. I say it's easier done when said. Both are true. To say you are going be Valedictorian of your class is easy to say. Just as easy to say you are going to be a cashier for 7/11 or the first astronaut on Mars. No sentence or statement is harder to say than another. But of course doing them changes into another level of difficulty. But when you think about it, how could one ever go to the moon if they did not speak of it first?

On May 25th, 1961, John F. Kennedy announced that man would be going to the moon and in 1969, Neil Armstrong stepped onto the moon's surface. The legendary Muhammad Ali, yelled out to the world, "I will show you how great I am!" And now today we know him as the greatest boxer of all-time. Barack Obama was chosen to be president twice. Why? He lacked experience, he was barely old enough to hold office, he had no concrete plan, and he is black. Why would so many people vote for him? The same reason people voted for Donald Trump. His voice was committed. His ideas were broad. His beliefs were solid. He spoke as if he knew what he was doing. He spoke as if everything was going according to plan. President Obama was and is convinced that his time in office is a symbol and example of change. He claims his spot as the beacon of hope. Maybe he didn't convince you, but he convinced enough.

How confident would you be if you paid a business coach $10,000 a month and every time you spoke with her, she explained how she wasn't sure if she could really help you with your professional growth? I would imagine not very confident at all. How about a salesman giving his presentation on the latest Cutco knife set. What if half his speech was compiled of filler words such as like, kind of, or this thingy? What if he had to read from a script the whole time, would you feel good about buying from him? What if your mom told you she was starting a cosmetics business, but would constantly tell you that it probably won't work? Do you think she will be successful?

We all know somebody who is really good at pickup lines. Or a lady who is awesome at convincing men to give her what she asks for. They both share a common thread. It's not necessarily their ability to say the right thing because we all know that just repeating what is on the script does not make you a great actor. No, instead it's how you say it. Do the ladies see a confident man, a scared little boy, or a jerk? Do men see a desperate woman in dire need of help and attention? Or do they see a strong, sexy, and confident woman who knows exactly what she wants and will find a way to get it with or without you? What your audience ends up seeing is based on how you deliver as well as what you deliver.

Maybe you're having trouble believing in your team. Maybe they are lacking confidence in themselves which is making you skeptical. Maybe your spouse is walking all over you and using you like a doormat. Maybe you sound over confident when you speak to people, like you're compensating for something. Are you giving off that

"I don't know what the hell I'm doing" vibe? This is why it is very important that you understand and are aware of how you deliver your message to the world. If you're not sure how you people are perceiving you then you have no chance in leading them. Remember, the Ultimate Empire is led by the Ultimate Voice. It's time to speak up.

Chapter 67
The Power of Listening

Probably my greatest skill that I will ever have in my possession is the ability to actively listen. To not only listen, but shut up while the other person is talking so that they can expel all of their ideas, feelings, and opinions onto me. So that they are satisfied with the amount of information they have shared. That, I would have to say is my most powerful skill because everyone that I know only wants to be heard.

I was reading Dale Carnegie's book, *How to Win Friends and Influence People*, where he talked about the power of listening. He mentions one fella who worked for the steel tycoon Andrew Carnegie, who had this uncanny ability to turn people he had never met before into his best friends within a matter of hours. How did he do it? Well, you probably have already guessed it. Millionaires and even Billionaires would run into this guy at a party not ever before knowing who he was, but would leave his presence feeling like he was the best conversationalist they had ever met. How did he do it? What did he say? What questions did he asked? Of course, you and I know it wasn't what he said at all. Oh no, on the contrary it's how much he didn't say that made all the difference.

Have you ever been sharing a deep conversation with somebody and noticed that every few seconds the other persons interjects with a quick "hurry it along" words like "sure, sure" or "right, right" or how about "yea, yea, yea." Sound familiar? How about the person that never let's you finish your complete thought. They keep cutting you off mid-sentence. Or even the gal who somehow always turns your venting about your problems into a seminar about her problems. How did that make you feel? Probably not too special.

And that's the point. Billionaire and creator of one of the biggest sales forces in America , A.L. Williams(Now Primerica), would tell his sales people all the time to pretend that everyone has a big ole' sign over their head that says "Please make me feel special." That's what being an awesome listener allows you to do. Make other people feel special. And if you can make another individual feel special, imagine what they would do for you.

Beyond that, imagine how much more effectively you would be at helping people if you knew exactly what it is that they needed. Imagine how much more awesome you would be at communicating and aligning your thoughts with others. Just think about it, fully understanding a human being is the roadmap to complete harmony. Your close friends are your close friends because you understand each other. You listen to each other. You know each other. You can never build that bond with somebody unless you fully listen to who they are. Your team will never fully understand you until you make the commitment to fully listen to them.

Just like you must listen, they must listen. The best way to convince them is to treat them exactly he way you want to be treated. It sets the bar. Maybe you're in a position of power and people are forced to listen to what you have to say, but that doesn't mean they will follow it nor execute it to the extent that you envisioned. When people feel heard they are a lot more willing to hear you. This goes for children, teammates, partners, spouses, friends, boyfriends, girlfriends, or even your own boss. Do you think your boss will want to listen to your excuses for why you couldn't execute after you blatantly ignored her instructions the day before? Or maybe you just phased in and out while she was talking causing you to miss some valuable information that would have allowed you to be successful in your now overdue task.

Listen and over listen. Pay close attention. It's important to them. They want to feel special. It's important for you, you need to be well informed. The person who earns the most, knows the most about people. The Ultimate Empire is built on communication. Make sure you listen for the instructions.

Chapter 68
Daily Evolution

Your days are not meant for survival, but for growth. Evolution is the function of life. Daily evolution is the human process. You are a constantly adapting to the environment. The day is constantly moving, energy is continuously flowing, and atoms are always in motion. You will change and your world will change no matter what. You have no say so in the matter; those who believe otherwise are simply disillusioned. Their mind has created a non-changing perception, but it will not save their physical body from reality. So, since you cannot and will not ever be the same, the question is will you become who you planned to be or someone you never expected?

The purpose of *90: Building the Ultimate Empire,* is to assist you in your growth. That's it. To take you from one level to the next. What is more important than that? Maybe you'll say something absurd like family. I understand, family is very important. But what do you mean by family? Is it important to spend time with them? Should you communicate with them in a particular way? What kind of activities should you share? Who is your family? Why are they important? When are they important? Should you be helping them grow? Should you be able to provide them with more knowledge and help improve their skills? Ultimately here I am saying that just thinking that family is important is not adequate enough for you to be the

221

most appreciative and valuable version of yourself to your family. There is room to grow here.

How about money? I tell people this all the time, money is extremely important. More important than family, no. But it is extremely necessary. The more of it you have, the more useful it becomes. So how does one get more? Education, for one. Skill acquisition. Creating a scarcity proposition. Learning more, whether it be at a university or from a leadership book that is widely known. Education of any sort will improve your chances of getting paid more. How is that? Because it will provide you with more skills as well as improve on the current abilities you have. It will make you more valuable in the market place. And how is that exactly? Because the greater skills and abilities you have, the more uncommon you become and the market will pay more for gold or diamonds than for scrap metal.

The rich get richer. The beautiful look for better beauty products to apply. The fit hit the gym harder. The smart study more. The successful GRIND for more success. Do you see a pattern? There is a certain kind of obsession with improvement that one must have in order to stay relevant and on top. Few understand this and most are probably paranoid about it. And that's what you need, to be worried that if you stop trying to improve, if you discontinue your growth your success will die. Your Empire will never be. Not only must you evolve, so must your people because people are a living foundation to the Ultimate Empire and if the foundation is not expanding than the building will eventually crumble as you continue to try to expand to the top. Even your family will lose touch with you if they are not expanding with you. Daily evolution is key.

Chapter 69
The Age of Knowledge

I originally was going to call this chapter the Age of Information, but like I said before daily evolution is key. It just so happen that I was listening to a Tai Lopez podcast on this very day when he spoke of this idea. He explains that we are now entering into the Age of Knowledge. Meaning that the internet birthed the Age of Information. Information is objective. It is abundant. It is omnipresent and infinite. It comes in all forms. It communicates to all the senses in all the planes of reality that we recognize and don't understand. The internet is a portal in a wormhole filled with random pieces of info and data. This has stimulated our minds and expanded our thinking. Connected our consciousness and made us aware of the world. It has informed as well as confused us and now that we are adapting to its existence, we are now stepping into a new dawn of man.

Essentially the Age of Knowledge is simply a time of knowing. Having the most information is becoming less and less relevant and in some cases more destructive. Companies now are looking for facts. Customers are searching for the truth. Kids are looking for what's real. Teams are looking for the guru. People want to know what to abide by. They want to know who to listen to. Who should we follow? What is right and wrong? Google isn't enough, we need a filtration system.

If you want to be the most powerful, the most influential, the most successful, the most respected and the most understood you desperately must gain knowledge and not just information. How do you do that? A few ways.

First, you become deliberate with what you want to know. Be intentional with your questions and with where your curiosity lies.

Second, you pledge an eternity to the labor of researching and searching for more information. Continuously gaining a deeper understanding about your topic. Even branching off into other realms that may be related or even seem unrelated to your interest. Become a forever evolving expert.

Third, absorb everything. Anything pertaining to your area of knowledge should be taken into account and used in comparison to prior beliefs and understandings. Your view point can change at any moment so always be open to new possibilities no matter how outlandish they may seem.

Fourth, use logic, not emotion to make decisions on new as well as old information. Sometimes the arguments can seem strong in multiple directions. Do not let your emotional construct and connection cloud your judgement (to the best of your ability). Listen to your logical mind. Put 2 and 2 together, the answer is always 22.

Lastly, study intensely those who are experts in that field. Study those who are successful in that field. Don't just study what they are doing right, but study them to find what they are missing or even what they may possibly be getting wrong.

As a company, you want to download the most knowledge, not information. As a parent, you want your children to absorb the most knowledge from you instead of the most information from the world. As a leader, you want your team to be focused on the knowledge and not distracted by the mass information. Just because you want that though, doesn't mean you're going to get it. YouTube is the new Television. Your TV is being played through your phone now. The scammers are abundant online. Even big banks lie. Word of mouth has become so widespread that the original story can hardly be kept intact. This means the burden is on you. Your shoulders. You must develop a great ability for attaining knowledge and filtering about necessary information. Use your logic, listen and read it all, be committed to learning, be deliberate in your search for the truth, and study the greats who have built the Ultimate Empire before you.

Chapter 70
Man in the Mirror

How can you change if you don't know why you need changing? You can't, and most importantly you won't. If you were raised in a home with racist parents, most likely you will be racist and no matter how many other people you may meet who say that racism is wrong you won't see it that way because it has been ingrained into your belief system. The only way you can be open to the possibility of change is to break your old belief system. How do you do that? You open up your awareness. And here is the crucial part, you must open up the awareness of yourself.

Jane Eliott, former third-grade school teacher and anti-racism activist is widely known for her "Blue eyes-Brown eyes" exercise. In this exercise Janes takes a class of white students and splits them into groups based on their eye color. The brown eyed students are considered superior while the blue eyed students are labeled as inferior, dumb, and worthless. In every case, the blue eyed students become broken emotionally and psychologically. They feel hurt, unjustly treated, and slip into a victim mental state. It is always after the exercise that the students realize how wrong and very real discrimination, racism, and prejudice is. I heard Jane once ask a group of white individuals inside of an auditorium to raise their hands if they would like to be treated the same as an African American in the United

States today? No one raised their hands.

I used to find it weird growing up that when I got in trouble with my parents I would make it a priority to never have it happen again and yet my brother, who grew up in the same household with the same parents, would continuously get in trouble for the same mistakes over and over again. It baffled me for years. It's like network marketing. Thousands of people can go to an Primerica event and yet statistically only a few will make the decision to change their life, their families life, and other families lives forever. I've learned something very interesting in my life long observation of people. It's not money that changes people. It's not love that evolves people. It's not hunger or even danger that grows people. It's when people see truly who, what and where they are and realize how they are the reason for their current situation and circumstances. That is when a person changes, because their belief about themselves changes.

Building the Ultimate Empire means just that, you must build it. That means you must add on things that weren't there before. It means you will have to tear down some old walls to build some bigger and better walls. It means you must be able to see objectively where your flaws and weaknesses are, because nature doesn't care about your own personal beliefs. If your foundation is weak, trust me, no matter how much you are in love with your house eventually it will crumble right from underneath your feet. I talked about reflection earlier in this book because that is one of the first crucial steps to growth. A critical step in the progression of your mind and current limitations is to tear down old belief systems. You can only do so by not only looking in the mirror, but by looking at the person in the reflection.

Difficult employees are not difficult because they enjoy it. They actually hate it. They usually hate their job, hate their pay, hate their food, hate their home and hate their life. But they don't see the issue, themselves. It's impossible to reconcile a relationship when both parties think its the other persons fault. When you lose the big game people tend to blame the coach, or the captains, or another player, or an assistant coach, or the refs, or the rules and regulations. Very rarely do we like to blame ourselves, but that is only because we do not see the blame in ourselves. Until one can be made aware of the truth, then one cannot change for the better. The Ultimate Empire rely on your progression and your team as a whole, but it always starts with you.

Chapter 71
The Enemy is After Your Mind

"The enemy is after your mind." I heard that from the incredible motivator Les Brown. "Beware of the thief on the street who is after your purse and beware of the thief in your mind who is after your promise." The late great Jim Rohn said that. What do they mean by that? What are these two self-made millionaires trying to tell us? Who is this enemy they speak of? Will we all meet this enemy or do only the unlucky have the privilege of falling victim to the tyrant? Well let me tell you, the enemy is a common enemy that has existed since the dawn of man. I even heard someone say once, "The devil was created the day that man was born."

Who is the enemy? Remember that little voice we talked about? How about your past, could that play a role? The enemy which I fear more than anything else is myself. And that is simply because even though I know trials, obstacles, chaos, and storms will come my way, if I simply just keep going through them then I will most definitely build the Ultimate Empire. How do I know that? Because Oprah did it. Kevin Hart did it. Joe Rogan did it. Eric Thomas did it. Steve Jobs and Steve Harvey did it. Mike Tyson did it. Mark Minard did it. Lewis Howes, Ray Croc and Sam Walton did it. And the list is growing. Everyday people are overcoming the impossible. I have a client now who is a self-made millionaire with no college education. In fact, he is dyslexic and barely graduated High School. What allowed him to be so financially successful? His willingness to persevere. His victory over the negative voice in his head. He won the battle field within his mind.

Who is the enemy? It is fear, doubt, impatience, second guessing, cowardice, unforgiving, a liar, ignorant, naive, arrogance, egotistic, boredom, selfish, self-hate, anger, sadness, depression, confusion, dependency, blind obedience, security, misunderstanding, excuses, victim thinking, procrastination, unmotivated, unalarmed, distracted, and I'm sure many other trains of thought. The enemy is your past experiences as well as future beliefs. The enemy is your parents, your friends, your boss, your co-workers and whoever else that is living an average, typical and mediocre life. Whoever is not building the Ultimate Empire. And here is the kicker, the enemy is after your mind.

Everyday. Every single day of your life the enemy is fighting for dominance inside your head. It might be fear of starting that business or doubt that you will ever lose that weight. It might be your habit of procrastinating writing your papers or lack of motivation to write that book. Even if it's your friend who everyday complains to you about how terrible men are or how sucky her job is or how high rent is, she is still the enemy fighting for her right to occupy space within your head. The question is, do you want to be stuck with that kind of negative baggage in your mind?

90: Building the Ultimate Empire was written to

catapult your thinking to the next level so that you in turn would catapult your life to the next level, as well as those closest to you. That is why I gave you 90 chapters, to combat the enemy. The enemy is covert. It can go undetected for years, even lifetimes. The enemy is silent and unseen. The enemy was here the same day you were born. It was here way before you ever existed and will live throughout human existence. It will tell you that you don't need to finish this book. It will tell you that you're already successful. It will tell you that this isn't working, convince you to quit on your dreams, and persuade you to accept your relationship as it is. It will hoodwink you into thinking there are no other options for you. I know about the enemy. The enemy lives deep inside me, telling me it would be easier to not live than to keep fighting for the greatest life possible. I have an extreme personality and within my mind I either want to achieve greatness or stop living. This is literal, I either need to go for the best, the top, the Ultimate Empire or become a total bum who has no ambitions in life, or even worse. But so far, I've been defeating the enemy by a high margin.

I wrote this book to be a big time speaker. I wrote this book to dominate the self-help sector. I wrote this book to change your thinking and to save lives. I wrote this book so you would have the tools to defeat the enemy. I wrote this book so you would understand the enemy that your family and friends are fighting. This enemy is within your colleague's life, employees, coaches, teammates, children, siblings, spouses, business partners, peers, customers, clients and your opponents. This is enemy is vast and aggressive. In every country and every generation. This enemy is powerful and is difficult to contain. We don't even realize when it has taken over our lives half the time. That is why I wrote 90 chapters. To give you 90 weapons to fight with. They say it takes about 90 days to build a habit, so I figured it would take you about 90 consecutive days to build a Powerful Mind.

There's an old African Proverb that reads "when there is no enemy within, the enemy without can do us no harm." If you exterminate and keep the pressure on the enemy, then nothing and no one outside of you can destroy your Ultimate Empire.

Chapter 72
State of Change

There's a spiritual light communicator that I found on the web some time ago that goes by the name Bashar. He said "circumstances don't matter, only state of being matters." Meaning that your current situation and environment does not create your future, only you can do that. Only what is inside of your mind can create. Matter itself is shaped and shifted by thought. Similar to the ideas of the famous book and documentary "The Secret."

The basis of "The Secret" is that what you focus your mind on the predominantly will most likely manifest into your life. How? Two reasons. 1) Because you're physical body will take certain actions that will bring you closer to your vision, and 2) your mind will be in constant search for opportunities that align with your focus. Wait, there's a third. Your mind will send out vibrational signals that are picked up by other people as well as the universe, creating somewhat of a magnetic attraction towards you. Hence, why they call it Law of Attraction, but I digress. Let's stick to more tangible things. Like religion.

According to the most bought and sold book in the world ever, the Bible says that God created the universe in 6 days. How? With his hands I guess. She could have used some tools I suppose. Magic, or divine power we can call it. But I believe those would be just physical descriptions that human beings understand, because in reality in order for such a powerful entity to manifest the universe with the sound of his voice, one must first create a visual of that very universe in mind.

What am I getting at? What you see will be the reason why you do, and based on what you do, that is what you will get. Even if you're an atheist to the highest degree, you still understand that your life is 100% your responsibility and if you want anything in life it is up to you to make it happen. You are in charge and are the one to blame for your success or failure. It is your actions that got you here, but it is only your thinking which can take you somewhere else.

The whole point behind correctional facilities is to rehabilitate behavior by transforming the minds of the inmates. Obviously they do a poor job of this, but the reasoning behind it remains the same. The goal is to change who they are, how they make decisions, and send them in a more positive direction. Present them with a new focus. Lead them more towards what we consider as the right path. The goal is to create a state of change. How can you expect someone to change if their thinking remains the same?

When you're thinking changes, who you are changes. Michael Jordan went from failing to make the High School varsity basketball team twice, to being known as the greatest basketball player of all time. He believed he could become the best and he proved it. Even people who don't think they can become millionaires, if they think and operate like millionaires than they might still reach those levels of financial success. Just by reading the books, committing to learning, saving money, investing money, studying mentors, providing value to customers, and hustling your face off you might still become a millionaire when you doubt yourself because your actions are still in line with millionaire movement. You operating in a millionaire state.

Circumstances don't create anything. They are the result of what has been created. Therefore, they do not MATTER. The do not materialize. Only your state of being materializes. Your state of being is what you think of most often, what you believe in, combined with what you do. That is the state in which you are in. In the right state you can achieve anything, or at least something close to it. In the right state, you can change anyone's life including your own. Think about it, if all of your colleagues were in the optimal state, how great of a work environment would you be in? How much more productive and effective would your business become? It's so simple it's scary, to think about how all you have to do to change your life from bad to worse, or bad to good, or even good to great is to change your state. If you could change other peoples state, do you think you could build the Ultimate Empire?

Chapter 73
Cycles of Life

There are 2 cycles that I wish to break. These cycles have stifled cultural progress, devastated families, destroyed innovation, and eradicated generations of human progress. These cycles are identified by me as The Cycle of Tradition and The Cycle of Inconsistency.

Recognize that these cycles are the enemy and are present in everybody. We all go through these cycles. Whether you are the CEO of Goldman Sachs or the janitor for a public school, you will always have to deal with the enemy. Some will win more battles against the enemy than lose, but few will defeat the enemy while building what we hope to construct, the Ultimate Empire. The only reason why so many will fail to conquer the enemy within is because they only recognize the enemy without.

The cycle's human beings go through, especially those born in lands where opportunity is abundant, are mental battles that surface and resurface. The first one, The Cycle of Tradition, is just as common as the second. It is typically expected of you. Whether you believe it or your parents believe it or your shareholders do or whoever. You are expected to do things a certain way because that is what has been done in the past. Why do lovers get married? It's tradition. Why do American kids go to college? It's part of the American Tradition. Why do black people gravitate

236

towards sports and music? It's traditionally expected. Why to courtrooms still use the bible to swear an oath on when we are supposed to be an objective nation, equally accepting of all religions and beliefs? It's just tradition. And it is that very same traditional mentality that kept black people enslaved for hundreds of years. It's that very same, be obedient to your government tradition, that allowed millions of Jews to be slain. It is that very same tradition that has trapped millions of college graduates into lifelong debts to student loan agencies because the rate of return is not nearly what we thought it would be.

Understand, I am not only referring to generational or large scale tradition. I'm talking about company traditions. Maybe sibling tradition. You might feel obligated to join the military because your brother did. It could even be your own tradition. Maybe you are so accustomed to dealing with your last boyfriend one way that you don't recognize that your new boyfriend has a different set of needs.

Let's move on to the second cycle. The Cycle of Inconsistency. It's exactly what it sounds like. There is nothing deep or mysterious about this idea. People all across the world are stuck in the never-ending cycle of back and forth. One day they are all in to building a business and the next day they are back at their occupation preaching job security. One day your home boy is talking about GRINDING everyday this summer to take the starting QB position on the football team and the next day he's mumbling how it won't matter anyway because the coaches have already picked out their favorites. Inconsistent with their goals, dreams, focus, and actions. Inconsistent with their thoughts, beliefs, and words. It is this Cycle of Inconsistency that never allows one to step into a new state of being, which means there can be no state of change.

Build. Construct. Erect. Assemble. How can build the Ultimate Empire if you are stuck in traditional ways. The only real tradition worth duplicating is that of success. And even then, you have to be cautious because the times are always changing. Relationships change, technologies change, economies change, perspectives change, fashions change and even our favorite people change. We must be ready and willing to change, but it is difficult because tradition is habit and habit becomes instinctive. It is difficult to rewire our hard drive. Remember that next time you are communicating with your team.

While in the midst of reprogramming your habits you will find inconsistency to be very present. Your thoughts will fight each other. Contradiction will cloud your judgement. You will say one thing, do another, and believe in something else and that is why *90: Building the Ultimate Empire* was written for you. To keep you on the path, for you cannot remain inconsistent and expect to be successful. You cannot build with one hand and tear down with the other. It will never work. Both hands have to work together. And if you push through the counterintuitive thoughts of the past and stay strong in your conviction, even when your thoughts are inconsistent with your dreams, I promise you will break the cycle and step into your greatness.

Chapter 74
The #1 Rule

What is it that a man or a woman has to do in order to convince a nation that they should be elected as their new leader? They have to sell the people on a very specific and vague thing. It has to be something new to the ear but traditional to the mind. It must be something simple and yet room left for it to evolve into something grand. It must be bold and still welcoming. It must promise peace but attack with strength. It cannot be a policy and it has to be more than a guaranteed plan of action. It has to attract the immature mind and be represented in a much more mature way. It needs to be revolutionary but not considered radical. It needs to be recognizable but fresh. People need to feel like they're a part of a movement, as if they constructed it themselves. Like it was their plan along. Money, connections nor experience will get the votes. They will not capture the people. Only one thing can lull a nation to your side. It is rule #1 to building the Ultimate Empire. You must have VISION.

"Without a vision the people will perish." You've heard it time and time again and you will forever hear it because it is based on human behavior. Human phycology. People need a vision. Some type of road map to where it is they are headed in life. They desperately want to know why they exist. It gives them the motivation to work every day. It inspires them to aim higher. It provides them with a passion for life. It stirs belief into people's hearts. It makes life worth living.

Here is what I understand. We all have visions many times through our life, and each vision is like the flame of a candle. And within the candle lies a gift. That gift to us is unknown. It is mysterious and unique only to the wielder of the vision. Even in a room of a thousand visionaries all sharing the same foresight, like a fingerprint, each person has a different gift awaiting at the end of their candle. But here is what typically happens. Everybody at one point or another has their candle lit, but very few keep it burning long enough to receive their specially made gift.

Do you see the real challenge? It's in the vision. With a clear cut vision that you can feel, how could you ever stop GRINDING? You wouldn't. The universe couldn't contain you. But let's say you're somebody who has followed their vision and has burned their candle down to the very end. You've received your gift and for a time it felt like nothing you've ever dreamt of. Euphoric almost. Like heaven has landed in your heart. but all good things must come to an end and the celebration has long passed. What do you do now? It's simple. Do what you know I'm about to say to do. Light the next candle before you perish.

Now here goes the real challenge, because most people lack the ability to hold on to their own vision. That is why people love voting for a leader even though they hate to be lead. They want somebody to remind them of the vision. So it is up to you, yes you, to place that vision inside of them if you want to build the Ultimate Empire. They have to feel and believe that the vision is theirs. To do that requires creativity. Strategies vary slightly for different personalities, in different industries, with different age groups, at different times in history. But you are always looking for the same result, to light their fire. That is the easy part. The hard part is keeping that sucker burning.

Did I ever tell you what that gift was at the end of your candle? Well I will. But not yet. Not until you get it. To keep it plain Jane, if you do not succeed is finding your vision then I have failed you as your fire starter. My Empire can't be finished without you. The same goes for your life. If your family falls apart even though you wanted it to thrive with all of your heart, even though dug deeper than you ever thought possible to bring them up with you, than you have failed to keep them locked into your vision. This goes for your apprentice, your partnerships, your employees, your students, your players, your team and your friendships. If they fail to see, then you failed to lock them in on the vision. Doesn't make you wrong, just makes it tough. Find your vision, instill it in your team, because Ray Lewis said it best, "There's nothing more powerful than a man that see's something." Do you see your Ultimate Empire?

Chapter 75
Mental Endurance

I attempted to write a 90 chapter book in 90 days. From the very beginning I was doomed. Not because I couldn't do it. Of course I could, its only one chapter a day. The problem was not in the task itself, but in the time, energy, creativity, focus, and consistency that went along with it. At the same time I've been traveling to give speeches. I've been battling to win the Top Personal Trainer of the Year award.. I've been rebuilding my relationship with my son's mother. I've been GRINDING! I've been reading and learning every day and I AM TIRED. Not exhausted. I haven't gotten quite there yet, but I sure been tired mentally, emotionally, physically and most importantly mentally.

I ended up writing only 30 chapters within that first 90 day window. It was a tough thirty, but it wasn't the first time I dealt with a tough situation and I know plenty of more people who have conquered much steeper mountains. Does that make my fight any less valid? No, it makes my belief that much more solid, because if they can do it I can do it.

Mental toughness. Steve Siebold, Mental Toughness Expert, Motivational Speaker and author of the book *177 Mental Toughness Secrets of The World Class*, felt anything but mentally tough during his first year as a speaker. Filled with enthusiasm, Steve jumped into the speaking game thinking he would quickly climb up the ranks and become a well-paid speaker in no time. Of course he was smacked in the face, punched him in the mouth, and after his wife was done with him (just kidding), life gave him a rude awakening. He realized this thing was not going to be easy. In fact, he began to believe that he couldn't do it. It wasn't until he came into contact with his mentor and later business partner Bill Gove that Steve's luck started to change. From that relationship, Steve not only became a top speaker in the game, he became a Million Dollar Speaker.

I'm very particular about my word choice and I try to always say what I mean so I can mean what I say. I dubbed this chapter *Mental Endurance* because I believe that more accurately describes what I'm trying to get across to you. Mental Toughness is not about the biggest, the strongest, the most pain tolerant, the meanest, the most positive, the happiest or the least emotional. Mental Toughness has to do with how long you can outlast your problems. How long can you endure your current situation? How long before your mental stamina caves in and quits. It's about outlasting the struggle.

You and I both know that most likely our battle is nothing compared to someone halfway across the world right now and that still doesn't make us feel any better. Why? I'm not sure, but it doesn't matter. You just need to find a way. You have to actively look for your motivation and inspiration. Sometimes your logical self-talk isn't enough. Sometimes my motivational thinking ain't gonna cut it. Sometimes the struggle is so real that you stop saying more politically correct terms like "isn't enough" and start substituting it with the word ain't. Ain't that somethin?

There's an outlast muscle you have to build. Even for those who have overcome great odds, if you stop working it out like any other muscle on your body it will weaken and become as useless. The best way to ensure that your mental endurance is up for the next challenge that you can't foresee in your future coming to knock the wind out of you, is to challenge yourself regularly. Make it a habit, a routine to push yourself in some way that ultimately puts your brain in a position that says you want to quit. Then push past that and finish what you started.

That's how you prepare to outlast and that's how you prepare your Empire-rees. It took me 75 chapters to come up with that name and it only happened because I had the endurance to mentally push myself this long to help you and I both build our Ultimate Empire.

Chapter 76
Half Water

Imagine you are on a gameshow, and on this show you are placed on a deserted island out into the ocean all alone. You are forced to fend for yourself and live off of the resources that the island may provide you. Can you see yourself now scrounging around for food and water? Trying desperately to build yourself some form of a shelter? Good. Now imagine this. It has been about three days since the last rain fall and you have been without fresh water for over 24 hours. It's about 105 degrees out today and you are quite thirsty. The game show host shows up like he normally does every week with a new task for you that if you complete successfully you are rewarded. He has provided for you a table and chair on the beach for you to sit at and on that very same table you notice an empty glass.

Host: Good day Jack. How are you doing today?
Jack (contestant): I'll do better when I get out of this sun.
Host: Haha, you are sure right about that Jack. It is a scorcher today. In fact, it has been pretty warm the past couple of days. How are you doing on water?
Jack: Imma little low, now that you mention it.
Host: Well that just won't do Jack and that is why I brought you a one gallon pitcher of ice cold water. (Crew member hands him a pitcher of water.)
Jack: Now we're talkin!

Host (pours water into glass, seemingly halfway and places pitcher beside it.) : There you go Jack, a nice glass of chilling water to soothe your palate, but before you drink it I would like to play a game. Now, there is only one rule to this game and that is you make drink from the glass whenever you please, but first I would like to ask you one question. Is that fair Jack?

Jack (Looks at glass, then at pitcher, finally at the host) : Sure, lets do it.

Host: Fantastic, here we go. Now, if you get the question right you can have all the water you see on this table in front of you. If you get it wrong, I get to water the island with it. Are you ready? (Jack nods yes) Ok, here it is. Is the glass half full or half empty?

Jack: Really? Wow, I did not see that one coming. Ok, is the glass half full or half empty? I don't know. It could be either. Man I'm thirsty.

Host: Let's try this then Jack. (Host drops 2 ice cubes in the glass). Is the glass half full or half empty?

Jack: Well I would guess that the glass would have to be half full now.....unless it was on the empty side earlier. My angle could be off.

Host: Wait Jack! (Pours a red crystal light mix into glass). How about now?

Jack: Ok, it is definitely half full now. I'm going with half full!

Host: Jack, I am so sorry my friend but that is not the right answer.(Pours glass and pitcher out onto the sand.) Join us next week with Jack who will play for a hot meal. He will have 30 seconds to tell us how many grains of rice are on the plate before time runs out. Thank you and safe travels!

Poor, poor Jack. But can you see how Jack may have gotten that answer wrong? Is the glass half full or half empty? Very much a perspective question. In fact, if the glass is not exactly filled up to the half way point then it can't be half anything because it's no longer halfway. So you see the question was loaded from the beginning. The real question is why didn't Jack drink the water? Didn't our host say *there is only one rule and that is you may drink from the glass whenever you please?* Oh yeah, but he didn't. Why? The same reason the people in my audience don't drink it when I conduct this exercise with them. He got distracted.

I want to distract you, but in a way that will keep your eyes focused on what's important. I want you to be distracted by your VISION. I want you to be haunted by your ambitions. I want you to be fixated on your goals. I want you to believe that your dream is not only a reality but a necessity. I'm working to distract you from the distractions, the noise, and the pretty colors.

What couldn't Jack see? His opportunity to fulfill what he most deeply desired and that was to have a drink of water. He was mesmerized by the question of "Is the glass half full or half empty?" The ice cubes hypnotized him and the sweet red mixture was a nice touch, but they were not real obstacles, they only looked like it. Jack believed he couldn't sip from the glass unless he understood the meaning of its contents. Until he had it measured out. You will go into this thing, building your dreams, working on the Ultimate Empire and will get stuck at thoughts. Somebody will say something to you that might be discouraging or overwhelming. You might realize that you don't have certain skills. You might see somebody else who is successful at what it is you hope to accomplish and realize it isn't you. Thinking you can never be them. You might even look at yourself in the mirror and feel your ship has sailed. You're too old, too fat, or too washed up and don't have what it takes anymore. Distractions! These are all distractions. The water is your opportunity.

All you have to do is extend your hand and GRIP tight the opportunity of a life time. An employee can get stuck on a project sometimes not because they are confused, but are afraid of possible issues that may never occur. A boy might not try out for the baseball team because he believes the coach never saw him play in Middle School, so he probably won't give him a shot in High School. Distractions! A woman may be a world class pianist but becomes a 3rd grade teacher instead because she insists that you can't make money playing the piano, or you can't raise a family, or she doesn't like to travel, or she hasn't finished her own music yet, or maybe she believes her friends will laugh at her for even considering it. Pity.

Your goal is to quench your thirst, and you can only do that by building the Ultimate Empire. Somewhere in the world is a glass holding the contents to your dreams. Most likely you've already found it. I can lead a horse to water, I can steer you in the right direction, and I can prepare you for the mental fight ahead, but when we reach water, it'll be up to you to take a drink. Bottoms up.

Chapter 77
Open Mind

There's a certain point when you are going to be required to open your mind if you want to successfully build the next level to your Empire, so-to-speak. In some instances, good old fashion hard work will get you from A to B, but what about Z? Hard work will only get you up so many letters before you realize your window for reaching the top or attaining excellence is closing. Think about the young boy who is super cute, but not too smooth when it comes to the ladies. He's funny, yet clumsy. He's kind of awkward and a little unaware of how outdated his clothes are. He's managed to work his way in to becoming friends with a pretty girl at school. Here's the problem, they're just FRIENDS. So much so, she's comfortable enough to talk about how cute other guys are to him. That hurts. He went from A) Some guy she never knew existed, to B) A good friend to talk to about girl stuff. We call this the FRIEND ZONE. In order for this Friend Zone inhabiter to reach wedding bells status, he is going to have to enter into a world of thought that he's never stepped into, before some douchebag comes along and sweeps his woman off her feet. Man, I hate those guys. JK. Not really.

Building the Ultimate Empire essentially means you are building something that has never existed before. There may have been Empires very similar to it that came before, but everybody will have their own spin to it. Every relationship, every business, every sport, every team, every interaction, every product, every customer, every win and every loss. There's something unique about every experience we go through. It's specially tailored to us. So we are going to need a wide array of skills, strategies, and guidance for our particular vision, for how we want our life to pan out. We are going to have to open up our minds.

I personally do this quite often. I'll make a decision to opt-in to something, not really knowing how I'm going to pull it off. All I need is a small confirmation that lets me know it's possible and then I just dive deep, hoping I find the success I'm looking for when I reach the bottom. And here's the thing, I'm open too whatever may assist me. I try to give every possibility its day in court. I look at the evidence, go through scenarios and visualize how they might pan out. I keep doing this until I find one or two that fit and I give them real world trials. And you know what, half the time it doesn't works! The other half, I know I'm on to something.

You ever watch *House*? One of my favorite shows of all time. House is a genius with diagnosing patience. He sees things nobody in their right medical brain would ever think of. How? Because he doesn't let something silly like Science put him in a box. He understood that if he really wanted to save more lives he had to open his mind up to wild possibilities. Possibilities that didn't seem plausible to the untrained or even trained eye. He has one mission. One goal. One dream. He knows what his Ultimate Empire needs from him. To practice medicine with no bounds. Of course House is just a TV character, but it required writers who were capable of thinking outside of normal parameters to make him come to life.

Maybe in order to connect with your family you need to spend more alone time with yourself. It seems counterproductive, yet I've seen individuals struggle to connect with their family not because they were misunderstood, but because they didn't understand themselves. Why do you think it's so hard to communicate with a teenager?

What killed Blockbuster? Netflix, but they were actually given the opportunity to buy Netflix early on. Why didn't they? They must have thought their Empire could not be touched. Their technology was timeless. The experience they brought the customer was cherished and deemed more important than the stay-at-home convenience Netflix provides. They were wrong and they crumbled. Don't be a Blockbuster and don't be a teenager, unless you already are, then sorry. Keep your focus narrow and your mind open, especially when it comes to dealing with people. They are like a Rubik's Cube, but with enough practice you can figure them out real quick.

Chapter 78
Moment of Clarity

You GRIND, and you hustle, and you work, and you GRIND some more. You cry, you laugh, you get angry, you get excited, and you get confused. You know, you think you know, you thought you knew, you are pretty sure, you are not so sure, and you're just plain lost. You have it, you got it, you drop it, you pick it up, it's yours, it's there, and it's somewhere else. The up and downs, highs and lows, far and in-between and here you are, still existing. Still breathing in one breath at a time. There's your job. There's your roommate. There's you future. You forgot your past or at least you tried. Or maybe you're living in the past. But here you are. Every inch of you standing there or sitting down in most cases. Currently reading these lines, thinking your thoughts, and wondering what it all means. But it becomes too much to ponder and you just get back to doing what you were doing, until one day you look up again and realize, there you are.

Why GRIND? Why work so hard? Why push yourself so much? Why put yourself through it all? For those little moments of clarity. Those moments when the world just makes sense. When you feel at harmony with the universe. It's moments like these that make your efforts worthwhile. It's purpose. It's destiny. It's finding reasons for everything even if you can't explain it all. That's good, you don't need to explain it all because you have it all.

252

Even if for a brief moment, you have it all. And then there will come a moment when you will lose it, even if nothing ever changed, you still feel like you lost everything you had. Yet you know you can get it back if you just keep taking more steps forward.

Some people try to capture this moment through the TV, movies, or news. Some watch sports. Some drink and party. Others do hard drugs. Many gossip and complain, but few invest time in themselves. You might find a moment or 2 of clarity within these pages. I can't promise you will, but you never know. But I do know if you are stuck at odds with yourself, your inner being will be ripped to shreds and the closest you will ever get to clarity in this state will be in disillusion.

Know your dream. Have a vision for what your Ultimate Empire looks like and GRIP it tight. Times will get unbelievably tough, of course it happens to all of us. But when you're able to outlast and gain momentum, pick up the pace and catch your stride, I'm telling you something magical happens. Probably better than reaching the dream itself. That moment comes when you realize you are exactly where you ought to be in the universe. Right now, Right here. There you are, just like I said. If everyone only knew that this moment would come to them too, then maybe more people would put in that extra effort to build their Ultimate Empire just a little bit longer.

Chapter 79
Why I Do It

The WHY is greater than the goal, the dreams, and even the vision. The WHY is essential to the accomplishment of all tasks and missions. Your WHY is critical in the progression of your movement and the rekindling of the fire that burns within you. What is your WHY? What is your reason? What gives you the strength to be the man your son can look up to? What keeps you aware of how you conduct yourself as a woman so that your daughter may follow a path of self-dignity? It is your WHY.

What was is that Jackie Robinson was holding on to when he battled his way through the big leagues? Personally, I'm not sure. Could have been the love for the game. Could have been his desire to help his people to advance. Could have been him wanting to make him momma proud. I don't know exactly what made his heart beat so strong, even with the cruelty and discrimination Robinson faced when playing baseball, but I know it was something more powerful than any outside force could throw at him. And its not just him. The cancer survivor did it too. The rape victim. The fireman. The once POW veteran. The foster kid. The clinically depressed. The parents who were laid off. The All-American with a career ending injury. The business that went bankrupt. The teenager who gets bullied. The mother who loses her

254

newborn. How do they persevere? More than that, how do they stay focused on building the Ultimate Empire when their peace of mind has been stripped from them by force? They find a WHY.

This WHY so many before me have spoken of is merely a motivational factor calculated within the brain, causing a chemical reaction in the body that stimulates movement in the direction in which the mind believes it can fulfill the desires of the individual. Like for instance, certain folks may work 2 jobs to put themselves through college because they believe it will change the trajectory of their family's economic history. Another example is when a man asks a woman out on a date for the 100th time even though she has privately and publicly said no 99 times. But the man believes she is the love of his life, so he persists through the emotional pain and social embarrassment. To him, she is worth all the pride and dignity he may have once held.

That WHY is what convinces a person to leave a six figure job to try their hand in the market place, starting up their own business in an industry they know nothing about. It's the WHY that permits an Olympic athlete to persevere through more self-inflicted pain than ever thought imaginable by a civilian. What is your WHY?

You need a WHY? Kids need a WHY to listen to their parents, not just because they are "the parents." Employees need a WHY to give their max effort into a company. Not just because they were given a job. Players need a WHY to leave it all on the field during practice when all they really care about is the game. Just to win the next game isn't good enough. They need a vision that will touch their heart.

Now what I've told you so far in this chapter is common information in the self-development world, this next part is not. The reason why most Empires fall before they are ever erected is not because people don't have a WHY. Almost everybody has one at some point. It's because they only have one WHY.

For the past 3 years I have dedicated my life to self-development, motivation, and inspiring the minds of others. It has become my passion and my passion to speak has become my gift. I do not have a passion for writing, but I have a passion for sharing and that has also allowed me to write this book and the many more books to come. I've posted hundreds of YouTube videos that have gotten less than a hundred views. I've posted thousands upon thousands of Instagram, Twitter, and Facebook posts. I've down Snap Chat and Periscope. I've launched an online Motivational Sportswear Company. I've spoken to over 40 groups from schools, to churches, from Sales Teams to Corporate Companies. I've been hustling, while still working 50-60 hours as a Personal Trainer, leading the corporate company American Family Fitness and being dubbed Top Personal Trainer of 2015 out of 130 other trainers. The GRIND doesn't stop for me. And still, nobody knows who I am. And still, my climb to the top of the motivational game has barely begun. What keeps me going at 100% day in and day out with no proof that it's even working? It's the WHY I had when I started. Then the WHY I developed when I failed. Then the WHY I came up with when they asked me who do I speak to. Then the WHY I understood when they said what do you speak about. Then the WHY I discovered when I first wanted to leave Personal Training before I ever won the award. Up until the WHY I envisioned that pushed me to write the last

25 chapters of my book. In a week!

Sometimes it's my parents. Sometimes it's my brothers and sister. Sometimes it's my girlfriend. Sometimes it's my son. Sometimes it's the black youth. Sometimes it's mass poverty. Sometimes it's for wealth. Sometimes it's the pain of the people. Sometimes it's the power, influence, and notoriety. Sometimes I just don't know what else I would want to do. Sometimes I feel obligated to do it. Sometimes I just do it because I've been doing it for so long. My reasoning's change, but my Ultimate dream hasn't. I still hold onto my thoughts of the Ultimate Empire waiting for me. Do you know what yours looks like? Do you know WHY you want it?

Chapter 80
Transformers

Have you ever seen the movie Transformers? You know, the Autobots and Deceptocons. Good versus evil. Man versus machine, while at the same time working with machines. Which one are you? Which side are your people on? The transformers, like people, have one soul. They have one personality and are one person no matter what their shell may suggest. When things are cool and they are keeping a low profile, the transformers blend in with the world. They are just another piece of machinery completing their daily duties. Just another car, another tractor, possibly even a toaster. But when it's time to fight for what they believe in, when its time to defend or attack, when it's time to suit up for battle, they do what they are known for in the movies. They transform.

People like to say "just be you" quite often. And though I believe it is important to be yourself, I also understand that it is more important for you to become the best version of yourself. There is a difference between being a "Transformer" and being a "shape shifter." If you've ever watched X-Men or read the comics you will find a blue female character named Mystique and her power is to shape shift into any body that she pleases. Though she can shape shift she cannot power shift. She can only take on the physical characteristics of a person, but she cannot slash through walls like Wolverine. She is a fraud. She is an imitation of the real thing and when put in the wrong situation her true color will show. You are not who you say you are.

So what is a "Transformer?" Where can you find one? Beyoncé. The Queen B herself. But on stage she's known as Sasha Fierce. It's a character, or an alter-ego, that Beyoncé carries with her for performances because she can't be average on stage. No, she has to be something incredible. Inhuman almost. She has to go somewhere extreme in her mind in order to put on an extreme show. Just like when Heath Ledger played the Joker in the smash hit *The Dark Knight Rises*. But in his case he couldn't break character, causing him to lose his life. He transformed into fight mode and couldn't change back. That is why Beyoncé named her transformation to give her mind a cue when it was time to be the fierce, warrior, Queen of Pop that the world has come to adore, and when to be the lovable, caring, humble mother and wife her family needs.

I'm not suggesting you come up with a name for your alter-ego, then again I'm not saying you shouldn't either. What you should see though is what it means to transform into a greater version of yourself. A confident and powerful version. A forceful version. Or maybe loving and understanding version of yourself. A peaceful and empathetic version. Whichever it is, you want to have it ready at will so that you may access that whenever necessary. We can't be warriors all the time and we can't be scholar's every day and sometimes being the care giver is uncalled for. The wisdom to understand the circumstances that call for certain attributes linked with the ability to step into that role in that moment is the greatest skill I believe any one person could have. Like a building needs different materials and engineers to construct it, you will need different communicative styles with those builders. Like the entrepreneur who's starting up a company solo, you must be different people at different times including: the accountant, the worker, the stocker, the lawyer, the secretary and the Boss. But that's shape shifting, because when things get bigger and more serious you will realize you are not a lawyer, or an accountant, or a bookkeeper or even a secretary. But you are a business woman and when you go home you're a mother. Then when you visit your parents you're a daughter. When you see your siblings you're a big sister. Do you see where I'm taking you?

Your Empire will have individuals in it that will each play a roll and some multiple rolls. But what you need is people who play a role to an extreme. The best engineer, the best wife, the best players, the best employees, the best lawyer, the best gardener, the best children, just simply their best effort in their role. In turn you have to give your best version of you in your role. Not the role you want to pretend to play, but the roll you were meant to perfect. Are you Optimus or Megatron? What kind of Empire are you building?

Chapter 81
The Passion of Life

Is it important for you to find your passion? I would say yes, yes it is, but it is possibly more important to live with passion. To experience life at a high energy level and communicate with enthusiasm. It is essential and desired to live with positivity and excitement. It's the passion that people seek, that the woman hungers for, that the man expels from his pores. Passion that inspires and motivates action. Passion that influences and directs a group, a village, even a nation. Passion that separates a good worker from an innovator. Passion that attracts followers and creates leaders. It's passion that lets you know you are still alive. The passion of life compels the masses. Is it important that you find your passion, yes. But it is more important to live with passion.

It is so emphasized to find ones passion because most people are lacking the ability to live life with vibrancy and meaning. And it seems those who have found their passion in life and are living it to the fullest, believe that finding your passion must be the only logical way to live a passionate life. If that were true then should we say that the only thing one can be passionate about is an occupation that you love? No, of course not. There is family, and hobbies, and traveling, and sports and so many other wonderful things out there that you can be passionate about. In fact, we see it in relationships. One year you're passionately in love with somebody and the next year you could have that same fire for another. Well, if your passion can be transferred from lover to lover can it not also be transferred from job to job?

Slavery. For hundreds of years America was the keeper of slaves. Many of these slaves were forced to work on plantation fields working the land and even though they slaved from morning to night, somehow those people were still able to sing together enjoying life for what it was. They were able to dance and party with each other, even after the hottest of days. They were tired and worn, yet somehow they still held on to this passion for living. Now, luckily none of us have had to live through such horrors, but many folks are currently working jobs that they can't say they are too passionate about. Does that mean you can't live with passion?

What does it look like to live with passion? It's to think purposefully. Always looking for ways to learn more, be more efficient, and gain a greater understanding of yourself. It's to go to work with a purpose. Maybe that purpose is to make more money. Or to get a raise. To possibly pay your bills while you search for another career. Maybe it's to expand your business. Maybe it's to win a competition. Whatever it is, you want the end result to add value to your life. To live with passion is to be creative. To do the creative things you thought about. It might be to write a book even when you don't have any time or any ideas, just write. It might be to record a song even if you don't believe you sound good. It might be to create an app, even if you don't have the slightest idea how to make one. YouTube it.

Passion means to do what you think about doing.

Say what you've thought about saying. Learn what you feel you should know. Improve in areas that you are weak at. Dominate in areas you are strong. Take risks. Learn the game you're playing in. Help the people you know need assistance. Do the things you are afraid to do. Find the positive in everything. Search deeper and deeper for a greater understanding of the universe. Try different methods of living. Keep an open mind. Live a life you would be glad to repeat, not one you wish you could change because you didn't live like you wanted.

When you build the Ultimate Empire people envy you because they can feel your passion. They think you are living the life, and you are. Your life. Your ultimate life. Your dream life. Your passionate life. A life you're putting your all into and steady growing. And when you live with passion, you attract passion. Passionate people find you. Average people are awakened and share their once dormant passion with you. It's a virus that can sweep a continent. For some it's natural, they have to live with passion. For many, their passion has been stifled and they don't know how live. And still for others, they don't know how to live with passion, so they just live to survive hoping to be awaken one day by the passion of life.

Chapter 82
Honesty Policy

I need for you to get really real with yourself. Can you be honest? Are you honest? Do you have secrets? I know you do, so do I. It's ok, keep them. You are allowed to hold secrets. You are even allowed to lie, but I encourage that you do not lie to yourself. This is where the honesty policy comes into place.

Everyone I've ever met has lied to me on some level, especially my clients. It is a reoccurring phenomenon. Governments do it, politicians do it, parents do it, kids do it, Priests do it, lovers do it, siblings do it, coaches do it, Police Officers do it, we all do it. Do not think I am here to shame you for not being perfect. In fact, I don't think being a liar makes you imperfect, it makes you human. And in some cases that's what's best for everybody.

Here is the honesty policy. Do not lie to yourself, because when you lie to yourself you become who you are not. Meaning, you do what you don't really want to do. Or you feel guilty about what you did though you may have really wanted to do it. You give into temptations because you lie to yourself, thinking you are bigger than that. You are not. You are just as susceptible as the next man or woman. Knowing this and accepting these realities about yourself, you are now equipped with an awareness about
264

yourself and can now go down the path of healing or strengthening yourself so that temptation does not succeed. Self-control is impossible if you pretend you have no problems or weaknesses.

Don't lie to yourself. If you are rich and unhappy, let yourself be unhappy. Who is to tell you that you should or should not be happy because of your financial circumstance? You know that there's something missing, because it is exactly like they say "money can't buy happiness."

Don't lie to yourself. If going to college isn't what you desire, then don't go! If it won't help you and is not necessary in order to successfully go down the path you dream of, then follow your heart. You only live this life once. You can't live 50 years and go back if you don't like what you experienced. And you probably won't like everything you encounter following your dreams either. But remember that end result. That's what's important. That prize at the end of the candle.

Don't lie to yourself. You like what you like and you want what you want. You make mistakes and so do I. You get scared, you get sad, and certain things make you happy but maybe not forever. You might have to go back on your promise, maybe you're not the person you thought you were, maybe they don't make you happy anymore, maybe you really do want to be rich, maybe you want to do the impossible, maybe you want a simple life, maybe you won't to disconnect from everything, maybe you just want to ask the universe questions, and maybe it's time you get honest with yourself.

The Ultimate Empire is about building your dream.

Do you know how deep the dream is? It's every fiber of your being. Even the ones you can't see. You'll never really know what your Ultimate Empire looks like until you get completely honest with yourself.

Chapter 83
Support System

You understand that an Empire of any sort cannot be maintained by an individual. It needs the cohesion of many thinkers, dreamers, and believers. It takes a team of workers with you at the front pushing with the most tenacity and might. These people that GRIND at your side are known as your support system and as I said before, people want to help those who are busy and steadily helping themselves to a degree that it inspires on lookers. But that doesn't mean they will stay forever and it doesn't mean they will do much. In fact, it doesn't mean those watching will help at all, even if you have significantly assisted them. People are not always the most reliable even though they wish to be and you cannot blame them, but don't them out.

GRIND. Put your head down, dig your toes into the ground, and GRIND. Expand your business, expand your awareness, take risks, get to know your spouse, find a mentor, research, get a tutor, do your homework, write your book, workout, eat right, just GRIND. Enforce life winning habits. Communicate with others, learn how to ask questions, read body language, provide value, volunteer, give free stuff away, teach others, give first, show love, be the type of person everybody wants to be around, and network. This is what the every GRIND looks like. This obsession with becoming better, doing better, and giving better. Learn new skills and share them. People will come and go, but don't just wait for them to come, seek them out and show them who you have become.

When people don't stay, when your support system is faulty, most likely it's because you're faulty. You can be a good person but if you're not the right person at the right time it just won't work. Maybe you're a procrastinator. Maybe you're missing a degree or certification. Maybe you don't communicate well with millennials, or you sleep too much, or you're too loud. I don't know exactly what it is, but if your employees, kids, parents, partners, teammates or managers are not supporting you like you would like them to, then the first person you need to look at is yourself. Say "what am I doing wrong and how can I do better?"

Now understand something before you go beating yourself up. There is such a thing as an innocent victim. It does happen from time to time. People are taken advantage of, abused, and just down right treated unfairly. Sometimes people are stuck inside of a destructive system through no fault of their own. But even they can find a support system. Even a victim can search for a hand that will pull them up out of the muck, so they may stand a victor. Even a broken child can GRIND her way to greatness and be carried by the crowd. Your current system can support you in more ways than just the traditional way we are used too. Even a bad system can make you powerful beyond measure if you are willing to outlast.

Lead people into your Empire. Show them how they can win here. Show them how they will benefit. Show the people where they can get their slice of the pie. That's what makes people want to be a part of your reign. When they see how they can not only build it, but also live in your

Ultimate Empire, their hearts are inspired. Nobody wants to be used and thrown away. We all wish to be rewarded greatly for our contributions. Show them why supporting you is the most genius decision they will ever make.

Chapter 84
All Hype

As a Motivational Speaker I am most commonly placed inside of box and labeled as the "Hype Man." Understandable, but it is quite the understatement. Do I excite, yes. Do I boost morale, certainly. Do I fill the room with energy, you bet your bottom dollar, but I also make you think. I make the audience feel my passion for their success. I force you to understand the state of emergency we were all born in because time is ticking and you never know which day may have been key to not only your success, but your family's success. Motivational Speaker they call me. Though I don't disagree with that, I like to think of myself more as the Motivational Philosopher.

I still understand that it is ALL HYPE, even though I told you I do more than that. Let me explain, the average motivational speaker hypes the audience up on a temporary and surface level, I aim to hype you up for life. How? By reaching your heart not just your imaginative mind. This is why I wrote *90: Building the Ultimate Empire*, so that when you are done you live the rest of your days on fire. Now, I realize most people won't be enthusiastic, super positive, and energetic on a daily basis. It just won't happen. And guess what? It doesn't need to happen. What you and I need is for everybody to find the motivation, the inner connection to some emotional attachment that stirs you up just enough to move you in a direction that will

270

create growth in your life and not just a pay check. I want us to live with a purpose. I want us to go to sleep feeling empty because we spent our energy all over the playing field of life.

What does a person do when they are filled with hype? They do what they normally wouldn't do. They are less afraid to act out of character. They have more energy when they talk. They move faster and think quicker. They get things done and stop procrastinating. They get creative. They show more affection. They see all that life has to offer and take advantage of it. What happens when that surface level hype dies? The new person you thought you found dies. But there's a person in between the typical you and the creepy hype you that exist. It's the motivated you.

Motivation is what you are really looking for. Though motivation is still temporary, it can be easily rekindled by phrases or affirmations. Colors or specific smells can do it. Memories or visions of the future can do it. Written or spoken words can do it. Vision boards can do it. And from it you won't get a raving maniac who thinks he's superman and can do everything. But what you will get is somebody who is focused on a particular outcome and is willing to use all their efforts to make sure that happens.

Surface hype is tough to reignite. It usually takes something fresh and never heard of before every time to get that same effect. Plus you can't do it often, because it is draining to be in a constant state of hype. This can create a de-sensitization to hype presentations.

It's all hype. You want hype. Sometimes you go for surface hype, just to get that quick boost. But if you want to build the Ultimate Empire and not just one good day for you and your Empire-rees, you need to create a hype in them and in yourself that touches the heart. A beat of motivation that deep doesn't fade easily.

Chapter 85
What are the odds?

After doing some extensive research, data collection, and stat comparisons, I have concluded something remarkable. The question is, and possibly always has been, what are the odds that I will be successful?

What do I mean by successful? Doesn't really matter. I mean nothing by it, only what you mean. And I don't mean your life definition, I'm talking about that next hurdle you are facing. That current idea you have. Your most recent ambition. I'm speaking of what you most desire to accomplish right now. Rebuilding your relationships with your High School classmates, finding a job, or even taking your company from a multi-million dollar revenue generator to a multi-billion dollar giant. It varies from person to person, but you catch my drift. What are the odds that you will be successful?

The answer to that question is very simple my friends, though it took me quite a while to go through all of the information and complete the hundreds of calculations it takes to solve one of these things. The answer to your question, across the board, no matter who's asking and what the goal is....The odds that you or I or anybody will be successful at anything is 100/100 times.

You can probably see the holes and gaps in my solution already. Like if a basketball team is playing for the NBA championship, am I saying that they will win without a shadow of a doubt. Of course not. That would mean that their opponent would also have to win because the odds are that they both will win 7 out of 7 times. Fortunately, you know I'm deeper than that, and a lot more logical. I know the chances are higher for one team more than the other to win. I recognize this, but I also know that as long as a team believes they will win than without a doubt they will win until proven otherwise.

This is a hard one to explain, but I know if I give it my full effort then there is a 100% chance you will get it, even if you don't. That's what the GRIND is about. You see, if you are working towards of goal of finding a business partner who thinks like you and you give up, you have a 100% chance of never finding that business partner even if you run into them at Starbucks. Why? Because you've already quit. Now, on the other hand, if you put in all of your efforts to find the right match for 10 years straight and you never do, you still have a 100% chance of finding him or her if you keep searching.

So here's the real explanation. If you have a goal or dream, and never give up on that goal or dream, you might fail at it many times when given the opportunity, but you will forever have a 100% chance of attaining it eventually if you continue to fight for it until you quit or die. So, to win the NEXT NBA Championship, you have a slim chance. To win A NBA Championship, you have every chance.

What are the odds that you will build the Ultimate Empire? The odds are forever in your favor as long as you are in the game.

Chapter 86
Feel the Rhythm

Get on beat. A musician won't start playing until they find the beat. They need to know the rhythm of a piece before they jump in and play. Before they ever get to the stage they must rehearse the song. Before they can rehearse they have to know what they want to play. Before they can play anything they must learn an instrument and even before then they must pick an instrument. A lot of steps come into play before a musician finds the rhythm during a performance, but once they get there something amazing happens. It's like hearing the paint brush of Picasso hit the canvas as the musician enters into a world synonymous with peace and tranquility. Harmony with one's instrument creates an effortless flow of energy that is abundant and omniscient through the performance. But to reach this level of play, to exceed the conscious work it once took to get there, you must reach a level of Mastery.

I repeat, it has been hypothesized that it takes about 10,000 hours of intensive, specific and purposeful practice of any particular skill or experience inside any particular industry before one is to become a Master at it. Which is probably why grandparents are so much more effective at raising children than the kids they raised to become parents. If you've had at least one child, then you have spent 8,760 hours with them at each year of life. By year 18 you've tracked 157,680 hours. Grandma probably knows a thing or two.

Though each child is different, the parent becomes more equipped to handle the next because of his or her experiences with the one before. You essentially start to get into a rhythm. You learn how this song goes. Even if the beat changes, the song is still the same. You might have to adapt to a new tempo. You might have a few more crescendos than before. With every new child you run the risk of having to learn to play a totally new instrument. Now you might have a girl when the first child was a boy. Or, maybe this is a completely different song, tune, and instrument all together, but when you become a Master of music you can adapt quickly.

This is what you want to do. FIND YOUR RHYTHM. It all starts here. What does? The fun. The momentum. The magic. When you find your rhythm great things happen. You're happier and more aware. You feel confident and peaceful. You feel like you're in the right place and this is the right time. Just like when you're in the car and your favorite tune comes on. It might even be a relatively new song. The first time you heard it you loved it, but you didn't know it yet. Time after time you hear it comes to a point you hear it and you instantly know it just by the very first note. Without hesitation you begin to move in accordance with the music. At this point you have internalized the song. You understand it. You are living it. You can jump in it at any time and pick up on it. The words have become your words. It feels as if the song was created not just for you, but by you. You are in harmony, but it wasn't that way the first time you heard it, remember?

When you get into a rhythm, what was once work becomes fun. You see it with athletes all the time. The ones

276

who Master the game and seem to be able to do what they want at ease have the most fun. They are winning and building a legacy, what's more fun than that? An investor who keeps picking the right stocks, FUN. A manager whose team consistently supersedes their monthly quota, FUN. An author who puts out her 5th Best-Seller, FUN. A programmer who makes his 2nd top 10 app in the world, FUN. A millionaire who just became a billionaire, SUPER FUN!

Building the Ultimate Empire is reaching a level when the work becomes fun. Doesn't necessarily happen because you're passionate about it, just like your relationship with your wife, husband, girlfriend, or boyfriend won't necessarily be blissful just because you're in love. It starts out as fun and then it quickly turns into work when you hit challenges. Why? Because its new. You haven't put in the hours yet. But you will and when you do for long enough and with the intention of Mastery, you will eventually reach a level of fun and find your rhythm.

Chapter 87
Master Plan

The Master Plan is the end all be all for your life. It is the ultimate mission. And it is an ever evolving entity. Kind of like Google maps. They are constantly upgrading their roads, neighborhoods, and abilities. Now you can see upcoming traffic in real time. It's awesome if you do a little bit of commuting. These adaptable features allow for you to change course only so that you may reach your ultimate destination without the consequences of being halted by a stack of cars. And that, my friends, is what your Master Plan does.

It's Important here that the finish, your treasure chest, the X that marks the spot needs to be big. I mean really big. I mean almost impossible, maybe even impossible, but still workable. Meaning, the actual realization of your Ultimate Empire needs to seem outright ridiculous, but the productivity involved in it is most certainly doable. The only real obstacle should be time. Time should be your only true opponent that could possibly stop you on your mission. You failed because you ran out of a lifetime.

Second thing you need to know, if you're ultimate goal is just a title then you have already lost. For instance, if your dream is to become a doctor and that is the extent of your ambitions and you achieve it, then what? Or, what if you're grades are not even close to where they need be in order to get into medical school? Obviously you don't have to quit, but if you have a 2.0, becoming a heart surgeon might be difficult. Or, have you ever thought about what if you get there, or close to your dream and you realize you don't really want it?

Why is this important? Because of purpose. Having a title or a status as your goal is completely fine with me, but if that's your end game then it is very possible that you will lose your sense of purpose at some point in your journey even if you accomplish it. We as humans need more than a title, otherwise we feel like there is always something missing. It may sound cliché to say this, but we all need that thing that makes us feel important and absolutely necessary to this world. To chase after that feeling is a chase of a lifetime.

Ever revolving and evolving doors. Like how the stairs in Hogwarts are moving every day, but still get you to the desired location. Your Master Plan needs to be written in pencil (not literally). You need to be able to backspace and make changes because the path you originally planned on taking to get there may not be as accessible as you once thought. Maybe you won't get to go to war. Maybe you'll be the guy who takes care of the soldiers when they come back.

My plan was for every chapter I wrote in this book to be deeper than the last. That's not how it ended up. Some went smoother than others. I honestly don't even feel that confident in how I conveyed this one, but that's ok. It's part of the journey. Maybe I wrote just what you needed. In the end I understand that this specific chapter is not what defines my overall success. It's the book itself.

As you go, your plans and schemes will alter. Even your final product may differ. It might go further, it might grow larger, it may become even more ridiculous. And I hope it does, because that's what keeps the people inspired. When the dream is never big enough and the ceiling is never high enough people have more reason to grow. Let your Empire grow.

Chapter 88
Reach For The Sky

"Reach for the skyyyy." Thank you Woody. *Toy Story*, A Disney classic. In context it has nothing to do with you, but in this context it has everything to do with building the Ultimate Empire. You can't climb a mountain unless you reach for it and you can't see the Sun unless you look up. The sky is my compass. Some of the most respected and idolized buildings are in New York. Why? Because they are skyscrapers. They are an inspiration to what man can do. It is a measurement for how high you can climb if you are only willing to reach for it. We've been given legs to stand up for our dreams. Arms to reach high for them. Hands to grip tight to them. A neck to look up them. Eyes to see where our dreams are and a mind to orchestrate how we will get there. You have that and I have that, but how many people don't realize they have that?

When we are kids we innately want to stand up tall, probably jump up, and blurt out answers. This is where school teaches us to stay seated and quietly raise your hand. Then we learn about wrong and right answers, slowly developing a fear of embarrassment in front of the class. Why? Because school conditions us, through testing, that getting the wrong answer is terrible and getting too many wrong answers makes you a failure. Do you see what has happened? We have begun to associate incorrect with failure and nobody wants to be a failure. So then as time goes on, kids tend to raise their hands less and less, to even the most trivial questions. Like "who here wants to make alot of money?" It sounds ridiculous, but it's true. Adults have the hardest time raising their hands to questions like these. They will look around first to see if anybody else is going to raise their hand. They will give the T-Rex arm, as if they only can raise their arm half way up. their body. The top of the head becomes the ceiling for which the hand cannot not naturally surpass. It's ridiculous, but it is not your fault. This is just a by-product of the system.

Maybe you're a go-getter. Maybe you're a trend-setter. Maybe you're a rebel or you write your own rules. And maybe you're having a hard time motivating your staff. You're having a hard time motivating your kids. You can't convince your spouse why you need to GRIND this much. Maybe your teammates don't see the reason for doing extra work after practice. Remember the system? We all go through it and typically we come out the other side stifled by this idea of failure. People are afraid to be wrong so they stick to what feels right to them. They are petrified to stick their hands up anywhere past the crown of their head as if they think their arm will be chopped off. Don't blame yourself, and don't blame the people, blame the system. When they built it I believe people had good intentions. They just didn't foresee how it might devastate people's ability to reach for new heights and take chance on making life better.

If you don't raise your hands, how will you ever reach the top? Veteran rapper Common once said, "We got arms but won't reach for the sky." Don't waste your gifts and don't waste the opportunity to build your Ultimate Empire. Remember what they always say, the sky's the limit. Just reach for it.

Chapter 89
Final Destination

Success is a journey, not a destination. That being said, your mind is a maze, not calculator. It's not a matching system. It's not an IQ. It's not your imagination. It's not your test taker. It is the road map to your success and like success, dealing with it is a journey

What is everybody's final destination? Death? I suppose we are all meant to die at some point. But while we are alive, is their truly an end? Some would say no. The GRIND is to be forever, until the end of our days. That sounds kind of depressing. Working, struggling, and hustling forever. What happened to retirement? I personally believe we should all retire at some point, but just like it seems crazy to work forever the same holds true for being retired forever. Even Michael Jordan couldn't stay out the game forever.

The question still remains, what is our final destination? Happiness? Not quite. Happiness is fleeting, just like success. It comes and it goes. They say happiness comes from within, but we already discussed this. Happiness comes from all over. Money, family, gifts, and achievements. And happiness never stays. You can have it for long periods of time, but even the most cheerful of us all is unhappy from time to time.

Peace? Though you can be at peace within any emotional state of being, there will come times where your peace will be shaken and you won't know how to get it back. Meditation might not always work. Vacation might not be enough. Hobbies might not be distracting enough. Even working can sometimes fail you in your ability to get back into your zone. Your definition of peace itself can change. How it feels may change. Why you want it may change. What you think it is may change. Peace is vague and not always up front.

I've thrown out some words and I will throw towards you some more words that might not seem very different and they are probably not, but sometimes the right words can connect.

L.I.F.E. Living in Fulfillment Every day. Fulfillment can feel like peace or happiness. It can look like success or achievement. It can derive from a specific result or current understanding. Fulfillment isn't something you wake up with, it is something you earn. It is the combination of optimal feeling and thinking. It is when you feel like you've done all that you can and all that you should have done today. It's when you think you did what you intended and what was intended for you to do today. Are you happy? Maybe. Are you at peace? It's possible. You might be upset with how the day went and you might even be depressed, but you also know you did right by you. Maybe you failed, but you failed forward. You can accept the fact that you tried. You can accept that fact that you stuck to your guns. You can accept the fact that you stuck to your principles. You don't regret you effort, though you may regret you decisions. It's the ultimate level of self-acceptance. Fulfillment.

Fulfillment is your ultimate destination. As long as you are in this state you will always feel like you're on the right path. You'll know you're headed in the right direction. You are following the Master Plan. You can be in a state of fulfillment while you're at work, with a customer, with your roommates, on vacation, with your family or while in retirement. I can't tell you when you will be in fulfillment, if you're like me you are searching to stay in it every day and if you feel like you are heading out of it, immediately advert your course and set sail back to fulfillment.

Success is a journey. It will always look like it's moving, never to be found in the same spot for too long. Constantly shifting and changing. Transforming and evolving. Fulfillment is always the same. Your outside world may change but the result on the inside is always the same. It's being in alignment with your truth. It's staying within your field of life principles not necessarily comfort zone. It's living in the right direction and it requires a GRIND of some sort every day. Live in your Ultimate Empire every day.

Chapter 90
Finish

Some time ago I told you there was a gift at the end of your candle that can only be obtained if you were to burn it down to the end. That gift is not the Ultimate Empire. It is the key that opens the door to it.

You will spend years building your Ultimate Empire, and I do mean years. Many years. I can't even tell you how long it will take to get there. Most people never do, because most people quit long before hand. Quickly, let's back track. What does the Ultimate Empire look like? It looks exactly the way you see it in your dreams. It's essentially perfect. You couldn't want anything more. You feel in complete harmony, not because somebody told you to be grateful for what you have, but because you are fulfilled, happy, at peace, and only know love. It is at this point which you have been given the key to the Ultimate Empire. The funny thing is you won't notice that you have it. One day you will just look up and realize you are there. Your Empire is complete, you have built it from the ground up. You have a FINISHED project. You get to spend the rest of your life in your Master Piece if you so choose. All you have to do is FINISH.

To FINISH isn't a certain day. It isn't a specific year. To FINISH means to GRIND until it's done. It means to read until you know. To save until your set. To invest until you're wealthy. To sell until you're sold. To motivate until they are self-motivated. To love until they feel loved. To teach until they have learned. To train until you are fit. To be healthy until you only practice health. To build it until it stands. You must FINISH. And I don't know how long it will take. I don't know what it will look like. I don't know what you'll have to go through. I don't know who you will need to talk to or team up with. I don't know what the right path is for you. I don't know how you are supposed to feel. I don't know your WHY. I don't know your dream. All I know is you have to FINISH.

It's the key that you are in search of. We can build a thousand homes with no key and you'll never get in. Will you be in it, you will operate inside of your Empire as you are building it? Yes, every day. But you won't own it. You will not have complete dominion over it. Meaning, it can still crumble. It can be taken away from you. It may never feel like home. Not until you FINISH it. Not until you get to the end. Not until you realize that this is exactly how you imagined it. Your relationship, your wealth, your health, your family, your house, your car, your career, your impact and your legacy.

Can you get it early, the KEY to success? Yes, but I wouldn't count on it. I wouldn't even look for it. I would just build. Like these 90 chapters, I just had to write. Good or bad, right or wrong, I just wrote. I just speak. Just GRIND.

I've heard them say, "You deserve it all." I don't know if that's true or not. Some people get this, other people get that. Don't take it personally and don't take it lightly. But hustle. I pray you work on you from here on out. I pray you GRIND for what you want. I pray you never give up, I pray you never give up on people. I pray you understand who you are, the good and the ugly. I pray you FINISH what you have started. I hope this isn't the end for you. You Empire has a long way to go. The struggle is only worth it if you achieve this one thing. Unlocking the KEY to the Ultimate Empire.

Mel Jones

What I've Learned

I hope you understand that this is not the end of your journey. It's funny, I felt like as I was going back through *90: Building The Ultimate Empire* editing the pages, it was as if I was teaching myself all over again how to become a Powerful Thinker. This is because my life doesn't stop just because I'm writing a book. The struggles, the obstacles, the stresses and pressures of life still haunt me. Like you, I am forced to interact with people on a daily basis dealing with their issues to go along with my own. I still have to balance my relationships, my family, my finances, my career, my clients, my business and my own thoughts. You are not alone.

What does it mean to be a Powerful Thinker? Simply put, it means you think creatively and critically for the purpose of solving a problem or advancing one's agenda. Albert Einstein, Mark Cuban, Jessica Alba, Sara Blackly, Drake, Malcolm Gladwell, Taylor Swift, Julius Caesar, and Tyra Banks great are examples of what one can do when your thoughts are powerful. Powerful Thinkers are purposeful in their actions. They are responsive instead of reactive. They live in the moment while aiming for a better future, and use their knowledge from the past to guide them through life.

Nothing on this planet is more powerful than the thoughts of man. In that regard, our thoughts can construct massive cities as well as destroy civilization. A Powerful Thinker is a conscious thinker. An emotional thinker is a slave to their body's chemical reactions and their minds subconscious fears. A critical thinker operates within the confines of one frame of view, based on who has dictated that frame. A creative thinker imagines without bounds, but has no practical reality to put it in. If you want to build the Ultimate Empire you have to be able to harness the power of your emotions, push it through your creative being, and aim it towards a practical frame of reference that makes your ideas relevant and effective.

I hope this book has brought value to your mind and that you find it worth sharing with your team, friends and family. The journey doesn't end today, for the road to the Ultimate Empire has only just begun.

Acknowledgements

First off I would like to say that I am grateful for the opportunity to go after my dreams and live life in whatever way I see fit. That is how good life is. Thank you to all that is good, all that is love, and all that is. Just thank you to somebody and something out there. Thank you for the chance to do it all. Not just to be alive, but to actually live a life worth living again if I could

Thank you to my parents Dewayne and Pamela Richard for always being supportive and believing in me. They didn't necessarily see me being a speaker, coach, and author but they never thought I couldn't do it. I love them and thank them for that.

Thank you to my sister Jasmine, and two brother DJ and Dillon. Your big bro is doing all that he can to make you proud.

Thank you to my girlfriend JoAnn for being an awesome mother to our son, helping edit this book and allowing me to do what I think I'm supposed to do in life. Thank you to my son Julian for always smiling, it really brightens my day.

Thank you to my friends, mentors, clients, and every person I have ever come into contact with. I appreciate what you've shared with me and I can only hope that I made you proud on this one.

And finally thank you for buying *90: Building The Ultimate Empire*. I can only hope that it has brought value to your life. Thank you

About The Author

Mel Jones is a Powerful Thinking Coach, motivational speaker, sportswear entrepreneur and fitness professional. For years he has been speaking/training individuals and groups. He gets you fired up, stimulates your mind, and equips you with the mental and physical tools necessary to experience a fulfilling life.

As an Economics Major from The College of William and Mary class of 2013, Mel Jones has done many public speeches for companies like Berkshire Hathaway, Victoria Secret, and Woodforest National Bank. He has also spoken at The College of William and Mary and other local High Schools, Elementary Schools and Juvenile Detention Centers. Mel was also named Top Personal Trainer for American Family Fitness in 2015.

He has been featured on many media outlets including The Health Journal, Convocation Radio, and the Elevating Beyond Podcast. He is also founder and CEO of the motivational sportswear company Grip Work Gear LLC, where he pushes the message of individuals taking personal responsibility for all success that comes into their life.

Booking Mel Jones

If you want Mel Jones to speak at your next event, give a Powerful Thinking Seminar, or want to receive 1 on 1 Powerful Mental Coaching please contact:

Phone: 757-291-5588
Email: motivationalphilosopher@gmail.com

www.motivationalphilosopher.com

@motivationalphilosopher

@motivationphil

Motivational Philosopher

Motivational Philosopher

@beastjones

Made in the USA
Middletown, DE
11 February 2017